ANALYZING URBAN POVERTY

GIS for the Developing World

Rosario C. Giusti de Pérez
and **Ramón A. Pérez**

ESRI Press
REDLANDS, CALIFORNIA

ESRI Press, 380 New York Street, Redlands, California 92373-8100

Printed in the United States of America

Library of Congress Cataloging-in-Publication Data
Giusti de Pérez, Rosario C., 1943–
    Analyzing urban poverty : GIS for the developing world /
    Rosario C. Giusti de Pérez and Ramón A. Pérez—1st ed.
      p.   cm.
    Includes bibliographical references.
    ISBN 978-1-58948-151-0
    1. Urban poor. 2. Squatter settlements. 3. Geographic information systems.
    I. Pérez, Ramón A., 1942– II. Title.
    HV4030.G58   2008
    362.50285—dc22   2007052630

Ask for ESRI Press titles at your local bookstore or order by calling 1-800-447-9778. You can also shop online at www.esri.com/esripress. Outside the United States, contact your local ESRI distributor.

ESRI Press titles are distributed to the trade by the following:

In North America:
Ingram Publisher Services
Toll-free telephone: (800) 648-3104
Toll-free fax: (800) 838-1149
E-mail: customerservice@ingrampublisherservices.com

In the United Kingdom, Europe, and the Middle East:
Transatlantic Publishers Group Ltd.
Telephone: 44 20 7373 2515
Fax: 44 20 7244 1018
E-mail: richard@tpgltd.co.uk

Cover and interior design and production   Jennifer Campbell
Editing   Claudia Naber
Copyediting and proofreading   Colleen Langley and Tiffany Wilkerson
Production, copyediting, proofreading   Michael Hyatt
Permissions   Kathleen Morgan
Printing coordination   Cliff Crabbe and Lilia Arias

Cover images courtesy of the authors, architect José Esposito, and DigitalGlobe

CONTENTS

ACKNOWLEDGMENTS

We are deeply grateful to Jack Dangermond, who not only offered us the opportunity to publish this book through ESRI Press but also profoundly influenced our view of environmental and social problems through the years.

Two colleagues inspired our work but, sadly, are no longer with us: Kevin Lynch, whose vision of the problems in urban barrios gave us a lesson of social commitment, and Luis Basil, whose unflagging pursuit of quality urban design furthered the development of excellent urban projects.

Special thanks to Elia Villalobos, who did an outstanding job refining the maps and graphics used in this book.

Thanks to our sons, Gerardo and Francisco, for their support during different stages of our work on this book. Gerardo reviewed the initial drafts of the manuscript and provided insightful criticism about the language. Francisco's drawings and survey statistics gave residents of poor urban environments hope for change by showing them the potential for improvements in deteriorated neighborhoods.

To our daughter Charito, always concerned about her parents' well-being and continuously trying to find ways to help, our thanks and love. To many others not mentioned here but nonetheless important contributors, our heartfelt thanks.

Finally, thanks to the entire team at ESRI Press, especially Claudia Naber, David Boyles, and Michael Law, who worked closely with us to shape our material into a book.

PROLOGUE

A STORY THAT BEGAN THIRTY YEARS AGO

This book is about using geographic information systems (GIS) in developing countries to identify ways of improving the quality of life in poor urban areas. We believe our thirty years of experience using GIS technology to manage urban problems in Venezuelan barrios can be useful in other countries. We have found GIS to be the best tool to help improve the overwhelming problem of urban poverty.

We began using GIS in 1976 while working at the University of Zulia in Maracaibo in Zulia, Venezuela. We submitted a proposal for the environmental assessment of a coal mine project called Guasare-Socuy, located in a nearby region along the Columbian border. This region, located in the northwest part of the state, had a rich coal deposit that had been explored since 1965. People from other regions of Venezuela continued to come into the area to work in the mines.

The university's Center for Regional and Urban Research envisioned designing a new town to accommodate the growing population employed by the mines. We proposed the development of comprehensive research to evaluate the building of such a town. As part of the team responsible for the Guasare-Socuy Coal Mining Environmental Assessment, we invited ESRI to serve as a consultant in this research effort.

For one year we collected information and created computer models on early ESRI software known as PIOS and GRID, working to identify the major issues for the environmental impact assessment. We completed several land-use models on the university's mainframe computer, an IBM 360/145 with only 512 KB of memory running Fortran IV. We ran the models on GRID software and printed them on normal line printers. These printouts became crucial documents for the assessment. This was one of the very first international projects in which ESRI software was used; in 1976 the software was not yet even called GIS.

Since then we have applied GIS technology to numerous studies and projects. GIS has been especially important in proposals affecting poor urban areas in various cities throughout Venezuela. GIS has helped us account for and describe the geographical location of facilities, land uses, and interactions in physical space. This functionality is needed on projects in both developed and developing countries. Yet the data that developed countries work with is usually much more complete and reliable than the data we have worked with.

In developing countries that lack services and infrastructures in poor urban areas, we usually have to deal with a dearth of data. Here we primarily use GIS to locate where community services and infrastructures should be located. In this way, GIS helps us to empower the communities that live in poor urban areas.

A RECENT STORY

After the coal mines project, we became involved in many urban design, planning, and environmental assessment projects—and we always used GIS as a supporting tool. We developed plans for cities such as Cabimas, Ciudad Ojeda, Santa Rita, and El Mojan, all located in the state of Zulia, urban design projects for central areas or new developments, and a large number of GIS projects. Some were implemented, others stored at government agencies waiting for political changes to bring them up-to-date. Nonetheless, all our efforts went toward bringing sustainable solutions to regions where change meant development regardless of any possible negative impacts.

Of all these projects one stands out: the renewal of Plaza Baralt, an old central square in Maracaibo, the second largest city in Venezuela located 500 miles west of Caracas. Our plans won a regional competition in 1995 and have been fully executed. What was designed and what we see now, though, have few things in common. In Maracaibo, where the climate is such that trees greatly improve living conditions, one of two rows of trees, meant to be kept in the renewal project, was cut down. How did this happen? Constructors didn't understand the maps. A knowledgeable urban technician that could provide adequate orientation did not exist. A lesson learned from this experience: whenever possible follow up on your projects or suggest the services of a knowledgeable technician.

The previous decade has brought new urban projects to the forefront, and planning agencies are aware of the need to focus on deprived urban areas. Competitions for upgrading squatter developments located in major cities are commonly advertised in national newspapers, calling planners to participate. CONAVI (Consejo Nacional de la Vivienda), a Venezuelan government planning agency, promoted competitions for upgrading squatter developments funded by the World Bank, and many urban planners registered. We couldn't miss this new trend that, for the first time, made us feel involved in projects that acknowledged the needs of largely forgotten urban areas. We registered for the first competition and our plan to improve Petare Agricultura, one of the poorest Venezuelan barrios, ended up winning.

Along with six other teams, we were asked to develop upgrading projects for barrios in Caracas. Between four areas of Petare, we randomly chose the urban design unit called Agricultura. Later we learned that Agricultura was the most problematic squatter development in Petare. CONAVI provided a general information plan for Petare (Plan Especial Petare Norte) that allowed us to develop a preliminary improvement proposal for the settlement.

We were impressed and disturbed as we analyzed in detail the aerial photograph supplied by CONAVI and as we visited the site. We saw a compact built mass (or hillside mega project, as architects would classify it) with very narrow lanes between blocks of buildings, stairs that seemed endless, and not a scrap of vacant land for miles around.

We were truly facing a challenge. The collapse of our theories and principles of urban design, used so successfully with formal developments, was imminent. We had to deal with a complex urban morphology, impossible to grasp at first sight, and with no apparent solutions for change. In short, our traditional planning approach was not going to work.

Many questions arose:

- ❖ How could we change our approach to improve this compact built mass?
- ❖ How could we approach this urban design problem using available tools and the written and cartographic information provided by the planning agency responsible for the projects?
- ❖ Were there ways of reaching the high parts of the settlement without climbing the equivalent of forty floors?

This was just the start of many questions for which we would have no obvious answers.

THE TASK OF BEGINNING

A key member of the jury was Jordi Borja, a well-known urban planner and director of the masters program on urban policies and projects at the University of Barcelona in Spain. Through his writing, Borja has become a defender of sustainable development and citizens' rights. To win, our proposal needed to meet the challenge of appraising the built environment and changing it in a sustainable way, which was highly appreciated by the barrio's inhabitants. Therefore, our main question was, how do we begin developing a sustainable proposal when restrictions and needs for change often are opposite goals?

One thing we knew for certain: site analysis was fundamental for understanding the urban order underneath that incomprehensible morphology. A standard map analysis would not function in that very complex environment. We decided to use GIS in every aspect of our project. The maps we developed became the basic reference for understanding the settlement and overcoming the inherent difficulties of the competition.

After we won the competition for Petare Agricultura, we won four successive competitions for improving barrios in various Venezuelan cities using the same approach. In this book we will share what made our approach so successful.

Our continuing work with urban and regional problems throughout Venezuela has resulted in a new approach to planning in developing countries. The road has been difficult, and we have learned that the great expectations that go along with solving a huge problem usually are dashed. A step-by-step planning process, starting with small improvements that acknowledge community values, and therefore pursue community support, is fundamental. We have learned not to expect that existing theories and full data manipulation can solve complex spatial problems. They provide significant help; however, getting the people who inhabit the space to participate is the key to success.

The required complements are tools that allow us to understand and manage the physical and social complexities of the underdeveloped areas of our cities. And the finishing touches for success are good maps that communicate at first glance.

1

A SUSTAINABLE APPROACH TO PROBLEMS IN URBAN SQUATTER DEVELOPMENTS

In developing countries, the scope and depth of urban poverty requires immediate action. Yet no sustainable solution exists in conventional planning programs developed by government agencies. Improvement programs that seemed to work when the problem was concentrated in 20 percent of the urban areas have shown themselves to be incapable of functioning in current conditions. Urban areas occupied by squatter developments in large Latin American cities can reach up to 60 percent of the total urban development. Today cities find it nearly impossible to provide enough urban services to satisfy the demands of the urban poor. Clearly, the problems in squatter developments are huge and governments are overwhelmed in their attempts to solve them.

To alleviate poverty conditions in squatter developments, we first need to understand how the developments function and how they are organized. This becomes a basic requirement for conceiving adequate improvement programs. In this chapter, we describe the conditions that must be identified and understood before developing an upgrading plan. We will go into more detail on many of these conditions and ideas in subsequent chapters.

SQUATTER SETTLEMENTS IN VENEZUELA: APPEARANCE AND WAY OF LIFE

In Venezuela, squatter developments, called **barrios**, are populated by poor people who come from all over the country, South America, and the Caribbean. Barrios grew as cities within cities during the boom decades of the 1930s to the 1990s. These settlements, ignored for years by authorities, house approximately 50 percent of the Venezuelan population. Figure 1-1 shows a typical barrio in Caracas, Venezuela.

Even though most barrios share similar problems, not all barrios are the same. The oldest barrios can be well-established with solid communities that have earned the right to claim government protection for their existence. An area with a long history of occupation is eligible to receive the benefits of government renewal programs.

The topography of each site and the dimension and characteristics of the adjacent city produce differences in the urban patterns of barrios. Settlements can vary from organized, dispersed grids to seemingly disorganized groups of high-density, piled-up dwellings. Barrios with a grid pattern can evolve through the years and become part of the formal city. In irregular high-density occupations located on the hillsides, the upgrading process can be complex and difficult.

FIGURE 1-1
Squatter development in Venezuela. Barrio Petare, Caracas.
Photo by authors.

Government plans for improvement

For decades, the breadth and depth of the problems of squatter developments have represented a challenge for government planning agencies. During the last twenty years, urban planners in Venezuela assumed that squatter settlements would evolve and acquire the character of formal areas once urban improvements such as building roads and infrastructure took place. In legislation for national, regional, and local plans, cities were visualized as a whole. No distinctions were made for barrio areas other than considering them as part of a special plan where the same rules and ideas for developing the formal urban areas were applied. Implementing such special plans usually required destroying the existing order within a barrio and creating a completely new one.

Examples of projects that have changed the existing social and physical order of the barrio are Barrio 23 de Enero (figure 1-2) and Barrio Catuche (figure 1-3) in Caracas. In 23 de Enero, the relocation of the population to high-rise buildings produced radical changes in the social structure of the barrio. Today this residential area has one of the highest crime rates in the city. In Catuche, a more recent relocation project had better results, but still greatly affected the physical order of the barrio. Replacing makeshift housing with high-rise buildings and widening roads disrupted not only the built environment but the social structure of the settlement. Sustainability requires change that does not disrupt the established order while improving existing conditions for the better.

FIGURE 1-2
Barrio 23 de Enero, Caracas.
Satellite image courtesy of Digital Globe.

The late 1990s brought a change in perspective. Government planning agencies, such as the National Housing Council (CONAVI, Consejo Nacional de la Vivienda) and the Institution for Community Development (FUNDACOMUN, Fundación para el Desarrollo de la Comunidad), developed a program for upgrading squatter developments

FIGURE 1-3
Barrio Catuche, Caracas.
Photo by authors.

called Programas de Habilitación de Barrios. The program for upgrading large areas of squatter developments was based on the following facts:

❖ More than 85 percent of Venezuela's population lives in cities.
❖ More than 50 percent of the city dwellers live in barrios.
❖ Squatter developments have a tendency to stay where they are, becoming organized and stable communities over time. For the inhabitants, dwellings are generally their only property, so they tend to protect them.

Plans to improve squatter developments began to be based on a more thorough and humane understanding of the settlements.

Understanding squatter developments

To understand squatter developments, we need to identify their dependencies and interactions with the adjacent city and review their internal physical and social networks. We also require a description of their origins, poverty conditions, and internal functioning.

FIGURE 1-4
Typical urban forms of hillside squatter developments: barrios
of Gramoven, and Petare, Caracas.
Photo by authors.

To describe the internal functioning of squatter developments, we need to define urban
fabric and urban form. **Urban fabric**, also called urban tissue, is the ensemble of aggre-
gated buildings, spaces, and access routes. **Urban form** is the physical layout of a settlement.
Figure 1-4 shows typical urban forms of hillside squatter developments.

A city within the city

Squatter developments depend on their adjacent cities in different ways; however, they are always spatially disconnected and formally differentiated from the city. Functioning as parallel worlds plays a key role in maintaining the social segregation that prevents squatter inhabitants from considering themselves part of the city. Instead, these inhabitants are committed to the interworkings of the settlement where they feel they belong.

Squatter developments acquire a unique urban character like a city itself. Visualizing them as cities within the formal city is opposite to the common view of marginal development used by most Latin American planners. "Marginal" implies establishing a category of location in relation to a center, where the margin is subordinated. This happens even though in today's big cities subordination to the main center has diminished.

Physical and social networks

Squatter developments can look disorganized and chaotic; however, urban planners need to look closer for evidence of an underlying physical and social order within the built form. Even if outsiders cannot perceive them, the internal connections that constitute this underlying order are fully perceived by the residents of the area.

The network of physical and social relations that inhabitants share and understand constitutes the structure of meaning. This structure, which creates the collective memory of the settlement, is a compendium of elements significant to all the inhabitants (figures 1-5A, B, and C). Urban

FIGURE 1-5A
Urban doors: Relevant urban elements.

Photo by authors.

FIGURE 1-5B
Urban doors: Relevant urban elements.
Photo by authors.

elements become relevant because of their civic role, dimension, or history. Significant elements, though physical in their expression, can have a social meaning.

To fully perceive social networks within a community, planners need to obtain information directly from the community. Inhabitants have knowledge about who belongs to each social group and how social groups connect.

Anonymity in city fragments

Usually a squatter development starts as an illegal settlement where anonymous individuals build an urban fragment in a relatively short time. Each participant builds his dwelling, and the end product is a settlement where public space is minimal and limited to narrow lanes or connection roads that access the formal city. These anonymous building processes produce large, collectively built areas of the city.

After the initial stages of development where survival needs are satisfied, communities cry for urban facilities and demand infrastructure. When city governments accept settlements,

FIGURE 1-5C
Urban doors: Relevant urban elements.

Photo by authors.

the authorities generally supply basic infrastructure like water, electricity, and, in some instances, public transportation. Providing and locating urban facilities is difficult since the barrio occupation process usually leaves no vacant land. The search for land to locate urban services constitutes the major problem that impoverished neighborhoods face. This problem is aggravated when the site has topographic limitations and the settlement has high-density occupation.

During construction, squatter development residents use a minimum of resources and a vernacular interpretation of the formal city codes. To mimic the image of the adjacent city, they may use concrete, build a fence, or install a glass window, all which serve as symbols of the formal city to which they aspire. Whenever dwellers are able, they introduce

FIGURE 1-6
Facade refurbishment and iron screen protections, Barrio Unido, La Vega, Caracas.

Photo by architect Victor Díaz.

these symbols that give them a new status. Through the buildings they construct, dwellers communicate their capacity and creativity. Examples include facade refurbishment and iron screen protections for windows and balconies (figure 1-6).

In general, when government officials target squatter developments for improvements, the squatters believe the officials should follow the same rules and policies they use in the adjacent, so-called formal city. Residents' most common expectations, for example, are wide roads that allow public transportation and cars to access the settlement.

Urban planning professionals must be aware that it is impossible to emulate the models and images of the adjacent city without destroying the organization of the squatter development. Traditional developing rules applied in slum areas generally fail. For example, applying regular two- and three-meter setbacks used in residential areas in the formal city would mean that many buildings in a barrio have to be demolished. To open the path to modernity in squatter developments, we need new and creative urban rules. We include many creative ideas for developing proposals and discuss them in subsequent chapters.

BELONGING WITHOUT OWNERSHIP

Communities in squatter developments become deeply rooted to the site where they live, developing a sense of belonging and territoriality. The sense of territoriality can be thought of as the physical and social knowledge that the inhabitants have, not only of their immediate environment but also of the surrounding context within which they move on a daily basis to access urban services. Whenever inhabitants become aware of plans for their community, fear of being relocated acts as a barrier to their participation and support. Barrio residents usually want the right to maintain their residences where they have their social relations and significant surroundings.

LEGALIZING LANDOWNERSHIP: A STARTING POINT IN THE UPGRADING PROCESS

Planning agencies have become aware that to obtain support for their plans and to guarantee physical, social, and economic security for slum areas, land tenure and home ownership need to be legalized. Only on this basis can the poor improve their dwellings and communities and acquire dignity.

Legalizing landownership is a starting point in the process of upgrading and will help bring about solid community participation. If the idea to formalize the ownership of land succeeds, squatter developments can become a great asset to the city. Providing home ownership will turn existing settlements into valuable real estate. Privatization will result in investments in services and infrastructure, and access to housing loans.

MANIFESTATIONS OF POVERTY

Physical poverty has multiple manifestations, some more significant than others, depending on the settlement's characteristics. Deteriorated urban scenes reveal crude images of poverty. Poverty is most obvious when squatter developments occupy hillsides and dwellings pile up in an indivisible mass (figures 1-7, 1-8, and 1-9).

The lack of public space as a basic commodity is a common characteristic of poverty in barrios. Difficult access to and from the settlement and individual dwellings is an effect of meager public space. Public space represents between 5 to 10 percent of high-density settlements. In contrast, the total public space in an average city constitutes over 30 percent of the available space.

Other manifestations of poverty include occupation of areas restricted for urban development, such as slopes with grades steeper than 30 percent and setback areas adjacent to water courses.

A NEW APPROACH TO URBAN PROBLEMS IN SQUATTER DEVELOPMENTS

Urban poverty is difficult to address and its continued growth challenges planning agencies that are too often ill-equipped to handle the problem. Planning agencies not only lack updated and accurate data with which to work, they also lack advanced tools to manipulate and manage information.

Faced with the challenge of mitigating poverty conditions, we realize that we need to do more than apply traditional programs. We need to collect information that is generally considered insignificant to planners but significant to residents. Gathering and working with information significant to dwellers, such as small places for meeting, religious icons, or posted bills indicating sector or passage names, makes a big difference. Sustainable improvement proposals depend on reliable and significant information from residents supported by a new approach to squatter development problems.

FIGURE 1-7
Image of poverty: hillside urban areas. Barrio Petare, Caracas.
Photo by authors.

FIGURE 1-8
Deteriorated urban scene. Barrio Petare, Caracas.
Photo by authors.

FIGURE 1-9
Deteriorated urban scene. Barrio Unido, La Vega, Caracas.
Photo by architect Victor Díaz.

Widening the context for site analysis

Planners have used and continue to use physical and demographic analysis as the basis for site analysis. In squatter developments, the complexity of the urban form and the network of social relations require a site analysis that addresses issues related to space and possibilities for improvement.

To develop sustainable proposals, we need a full understanding of the physical and social order embedded in the squatter development. Analysis must include identifying the inhabitants' structure of meaning and considering their sense of belonging. When site analysis places the squatter development within a context, we view the settlement as a unit; therefore, we identify the existing or potential connections with the city. Analysis of the interior of the development must detail urban form, memories and meanings embedded in the urban form, urban fabric, linkages between physical form and the network of social relations, and the underlying order that frames and guides inhabitants' perceptions and relations. To do site analysis of squatter developments, we need tools that allow us to manipulate and combine complex data to establish a framework for sustainable development proposals.

DEVELOPING A FRAMEWORK FOR SUSTAINABLE IMPROVEMENT PLANS

Sustainable upgrading needs to reduce adverse human impacts on the natural environment and simultaneously preserve the social structures and physical order. Whenever the protection of the ecosystems and the human value systems seem like incompatible goals, planners have to make difficult choices and sustainability is threatened. The ultimate goal remains improving quality of life.

What is the threshold for sustainability when improvement proposals seek to upgrade the quality of life? A threshold, even though ambiguous, defines a line where, on one side, the community's daily life functions, while on the other side it does not. To establish a capacity for change, we need to consider restrictions that are intimately related to urban form and to the underlying order.

In traditional urban areas, interventions to improve the quality of life can proceed until standard indexes are reached. To reach the same standards, squatter developments require radical modifications that affect their social and physical functioning. When changes affect the existing social structures and physical order, we reach the threshold for sustainable interventions.

Sustainable proposals supported by enhancing the urban scene

Squatter developments require planning that is free from traditional, numerical standards. Improvement has to exceed utilitarian concepts of efficiency and emphasize the embellishment and enhancement of the urban scene as a fundamental ingredient of planning proposals. Although actual improvement policies have given great importance to the traditional cultural structure of the communities, they have not established the need for favoring embellishment and incorporating civic elements in the urban scene. Therefore, when dealing with sustainability, urban proposals must include beauty as a basic goal. Initiatives for facade improvement, often promoted by squatter development residents, must be part of renewal programs (figure 1-10).

FIGURE 1-10

Initiatives for facade improvements within a squatter development. Barrio Guarataro, Caracas.

Photo by authors.

Preserving sustainability without public land

When squatter developments severely lack public land, planners can be tempted to enlarge expropriations to provide necessary services. Satisfying the need for services through expropriations and relocations, however, will produce radical changes in the settlement that will affect the sustainability of the proposal.

In order for public works to be successful, friendly interventions need to be incorporated into the existing built environment. Because the lack of available public land limits the possibilities for change, modifications of the existing built form must be insertions of small fragments of development. In the initial stages of a process, proposing partial or prompt changes to the habitat that are capable of evolving toward formal city conditions is considered feasible and sustainable.

The search for public land in these settlements must be solved with minimal impact on the built environment. With this goal in mind, solutions that use the interstices between buildings or any residual space for public use become one of the best options. This solution allows us to insert urban elements or activities without massive physical changes. We need to build within the built and establish new forms of land property, such as condominiums.

New development controls for squatter areas

Controlling urban occupation in squatter developments, especially those that have a complex urban form, requires specific rules. The irregular ways buildings pile up and the nonexistence of defined lots require special regulations.

Families existing side by side in attached dwellings benefit from the establishment of behavioral rules. For example, buildings should avoid balconies and roof projections that inter-fere with natural lighting. Dimension limits have to be established for all elements pro-jected over narrow public space (figures 1-11A and B). The use and care of public space needs to be a matter of agreement between residents. Behavioral rules can guarantee the smooth social functioning of the communities.

Novel solutions for apparently unsolvable problems

Problems classified as unsolvable are those that require radical modifications of the built envi-ronment. In squatter developments, solving problems related to accessibility to the formal city and availability of infrastructure requires nonstandard solutions that generally increase

FIGURE 1-11A
Arrangement of a narrow public space. Petare, Caracas.

Photo by authors.

FIGURE 1-11B
Arrangement of a narrow public space.
Petare, Caracas.
Photo by authors.

costs. Yet an increase in quality of life makes increases in costs worthwhile.

Figure 1-12 shows design ideas for elevated sidewalks, later developed as projects, to improve pedestrian accessibility. Figure 1-13 shows access stairs to Petare developed by the agency for community development FUNDACOMUN.

Tools for analyzing and organizing data

GIS provides a valuable set of tools for building what-if scenarios; developing models of the urban space, and changing the figures, amounts, and percentages that allow us to see in real time how the virtual urban space changes as we manipulate measures and proposals for urban development.

In developed countries, GIS has proven to be an excellent way to manage urban spatial data. GIS can produce beautiful maps of the urban geography, showing in vivid thematic cartography where everything is located within the urban space.

In developing countries, the story is different. Lack of data is the norm and it is difficult to find maps showing land use, location of facilities, transportation networks, and so forth. Statistics about population and socioeconomic activities are missing. Even more relevant, nobody is collecting the information. In poor urban areas, information is scarce or nonexistent.

In developing countries, the real use of GIS is to identify the absent or scarce social needs and locate them in the best available space. This approach requires a more intelligent GIS. We need to apply the technology not just for estimating what proportion of public space is needed, but also for sensing elements that are absent.

FIGURE 1-12
The photo at the right shows design
idea for elevated sidewalks to improve
accessibility.

Photo and composition by Rosario C. Giusti de Pérez.

FIGURE 1-13
Access stairs in Petare.

Photo by authors.

In developed countries, the use of two-dimensional GIS maps is more than enough to describe and identify solutions for urban planning. In developing countries, we need to treat the urban space in a multidimensional way. Visualization in 3D is fundamental for showing the complexities of social interactions and making smart estimations of where to locate community services.

GIS TO SUPPORT SUSTAINABLE ANSWERS

This book delineates an approach that uses GIS to guide improvement in squatter developments in developing countries. Additionally, the book explores how to collect data while analyzing and planning for the poor.

We propose the following rules of thumb when using GIS in squatter developments:

1. Create procedures to involve communities in collecting the information required for identifying their problems and opportunities. This will solve the problem of lack of data.
2. Use GIS to encourage community participation in this effort. Visualizing their own data in the form of maps helps residents understand their problems.
3. Create a communal GIS visualization room within the neighborhood.
4. Collect information about the population and its socioeconomic status and potentialities. This is as important as collecting information about the urban space itself.
5. Describe the socioeconomic data in geographical terms.
6. Identify the social relations and interaction of the population with the open spaces in the community. This is more important than merely describing land use.
7. Describe community relationships as schematics of the database showing problems and capabilities within the community to solve these problems.
8. Use GIS to trace the fundamentals of the underlying urban order in complex urban morphologies. Visualization in 3D is required to identify and understand this order.
9. Use GIS to show how the community uses a complex and sometimes hidden network of pathways to cope with the lack of public transportation and streets. Describing how each dwelling traces its access to the public spaces and to the rest of the city is very important. Visualization in 3D is a must for understanding this complexity.
10. Use ArcGIS Spatial Analyst ModelBuilder in hilly squatter developments to help identify steep slopes, drainage patterns, and accessibility to open spaces.

ABOUT THIS BOOK

The following chapters describe the steps required to develop a successful improvement project for squatter developments. We cover reviewing the natural and built environment and their poverty conditions, developing appropriate improvement proposals, managing these projects, and working with communities.

Site analysis is usually the initial step for planners. Chapter 2 describes methods to review environmental limitations as the main constraint for urban development.

Chapter 3 describes a method of analyzing the urban built environment in high-density squatter developments. Site analysis of the natural and the urban built environments described in chapters 2 and 3 entail the entire physical review of the settlement.

Chapter 4 qualifies the conditions of a settlement's natural and built environments and displays them through poverty maps.

Chapter 5 shows how to develop improvement proposals of the existing built environment where preserving residents' values is a primary planning goal. Chapter 6 describes how to manage improvement projects with GIS, and chapter 7 deals with organizing communities and encouraging their participation.

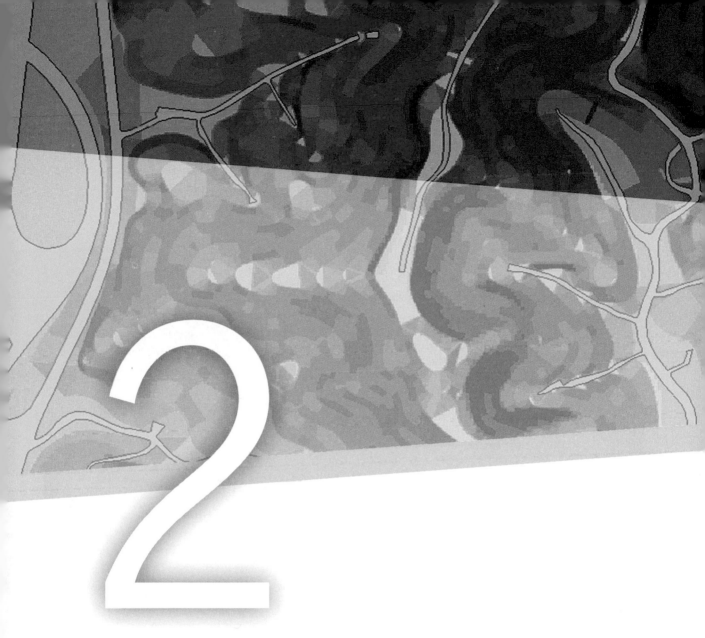

2

SITE ANALYSIS OF THE ENVIRONMENT

When developing improvement plans, site analysis is usually the first step, and planning for squatter developments is no different. Planners need a full understanding of any site's environmental conditions to establish occupation rules and to determine whether or not the urban built environment is adapted to these conditions.

Environmental limitations are the main constraint for urban development. Yet we don't manage these constraints in squatter developments as we do in the formal areas of the city. In formal areas, established development rules guide occupation and hence improvement. In squatter developments, the inhabitants' imperative need for land, whatever the environmental restrictions of the site, guide occupation and improvement.

Although establishing some rules might at first seem difficult or superfluous, doing so helps planners find answers to improve quality of life, especially when sites have environmental limitations. General development guidelines can help us improve living conditions whenever relocation is not a policy. Where and how development constraints are specially managed in these informal occupations is the topic of this chapter.

PROPOSED METHODOLOGY

Analyzing the built environment within poor neighborhoods in developing countries, and especially in some Latin American cities, involves adapting proven methodologies so we can identify environmental issues relevant to urban planning. Most of the literature related to environmental and site analysis focuses on information overlay that describes the behavior of the terrain at the site. Behavior for variables such as soil types, geology, natural drainage, geomorphology, hydrology, climate, and other biotic and geodynamic themes become the main issues. Comparing the built environment to the results of a thematic overlay of the site's natural variables, we identify areas of contradiction, especially those unsuitable and risky for locating human activities. Above all, overlay allows us to identify possible environmental impacts in the long run.

One methodology, the **threshold theory**, was developed after World War II in Poland. Recovering and rebuilding the massive destruction suffered by the urban fabric of cities like Warsaw required the development of quick recovery procedures. The threshold theory is a methodology that identifies borders, limits, and thresholds in land characteristics and in urban fabrics, especially in previously occupied land.

The Polish city planners Pitor Zaremba and Jerzy Kozlowski, who applied the threshold theory to city planning, concluded that it was less costly recovering demolished spaces than building new ones. Most of the urban spaces demolished during the war kept some degree of recoverable infrastructures, such as water supply, streets, and other networks. Because of the high cost of starting from scratch, the threshold theory proved to be the right approach for rebuilding most of the cities affected by the war.

Squatter developments can be compared to war-devastated cities, since in both cases infrastructure and urban facilities are deteriorated or do not exist. But because squatter developments usually trespass the maximum limits of urban development accepted in formal urban planning, we used a more recent methodology to define environmental constraints such as development thresholds. We introduce the concept of **ultimate threshold**, which considers environmental limitations as the only real constraints for urban development.

Ultimate environmental thresholds (UETs)

The ultimate environmental threshold addresses the regenerative capability of the environment and ecosystems and leads to the recognition of environmental thresholds, some of which represent significant and specific development limits. Ultimate thresholds indicate the final boundaries for possible urban location (Kozlowski and Hudges 1972).

Living in squatter developments in Caracas and many Latin American cities means living within a border of ultimate thresholds: houses are frequently lost in landslides, and roads and streets erode from open surface sewerage. Based on these characteristics, we developed a methodology similar to threshold theory; however, this methodology is adapted to developing countries and combined with modern site analysis tools like GIS.

Analyzing the site

The following list summarizes the information analyses that help planners understand the poor urban built environment:

1. Analysis of the natural features of the site. GIS can be helpful in analyzing and understanding the characteristics of the site by overlaying maps about soils, geomorphology, vegetation, terrain slope, and orientation.
2. Description and classification of urban site environmental problems. GIS can pinpoint locations and show the relationship between environmental problems and direct or indirect causes.
3. Identification and visualization of relationships between environmental problems and the social network within and outside the settlement. This cause and effect can be understood and described geographically with GIS.

4. Analysis of the different grades of poverty by classifying the accessibility of each dwelling to public services such as schools, public transportation, water supply, electricity, and others.

5. Identification of community groups and individuals who are affected by removal or expropriation of dwellings.

6. Identification of sites and spaces for urban improvements.

7. Support for urban designers in proposing improvements of the built environment.

8. Support for public institutions, local government, and community leaders in controlling and following up improvement plans and actions.

ANALYZING THE NATURAL FEATURES OF THE SITE WITH GIS

Because of a lack of data, planners use indirect ways to analyze terrain. Usually basic maps come from various sources and have differing scales, resolutions, and precisions. Overlaying requires that these maps be standardized, rescaled, and adjusted to fit with and recognize common borders and limits. GIS, however, can help overcome the absence of basic terrain data in squatter developments. Using simple overlays and relationships between different themes, GIS helps to locate and describe the behavior of the site.

Terrain analysis using GIS

In the threshold theory, the recommended basic data includes information about the physiographic qualities of the terrain that allows planners to identify borders and limits that support urban development. We also recommend data about the built environment and data about infrastructure. The main objective is to identify maximum capacity limits of people who can be served. For example, the capacity of a reservoir with treated water and the serving capacity of a water supply network have thresholds that can be translated into a surface or threshold polygon. Any population located beyond this threshold surface will not have a water supply.

We found a noteworthy correspondence between the threshold theory and the method for land analysis proposed by landscape architect Ian McHarg. Both methods treat physiographic variables similarly and both search for limits or thresholds in land behavior to accommodate types of urban development. Both threshold theory and McHarg's method propose a computational overlay of variables, discretely simplified to describe the urban space.

Squatter developments usually have little available information about physiographic qualities of the terrain, so planners need to design an information system that can operate relatively efficiently in the absence of data. The structure of the proposed information system must consider, at the least, the following subsystems:

- ❖ Data that describes the average physics of the terrain: land form, type of soils, and general geography of space where urban activities are located. This is also called data about the natural geography of the site.
- ❖ Data that describes the activities on the terrain: dimension, nature, capacities, form of arrangement on the land, and its intensity of operation. This includes land-use data.
- ❖ Data that describes the channels of interaction between the activities: dimension and intensity of interaction, and degree of arrangement of the interaction. This includes data on channels that supply service to urban spaces and connect the spaces with other units of the city (infrastructure and accessibility).

Terrain information

Terrain information is the natural physical land behavior data that defines and limits the site. A terrain information unit is a land unit that shows the same behavior as fundamental physiographic variables. The behavior of each variable is based on its ability to accept and accommodate development of urban activities; therefore, the analyses are maps that summarize, in the form of potential surfaces, the degrees of adequacy of each variable to accommodate urban development.

Zones that have the same capacity for urban development constitute homogenous units of territory. These units will become the "units of space" that accommodate activities. Space is then classified by its capacity to support or accommodate activities.

Terrain data includes at least the following sets of information:

- ❖ Integrated terrain units showing homogenous physiographic behavior that describes their natural capacity to support urban activities
- ❖ Terrain unit classification to obtain the following:
  - ◆ Surfaces suitable for urban development
  - ◆ Surfaces adaptable for urban development at some cost
  - ◆ Surfaces not available for urban development at any cost
  - ◆ Surfaces not suitable for development (available for conservation and environmental protection)

Evaluation criteria

Terrain units must be described in terms of a set of numerical or alphanumerical codes so that GIS can classify and present them as thematic maps. Once the land is described in terrain units, we establish a unit classification according to additional development costs based on land behavior. For squatter developments, we created the set of analysis criteria shown in table 2-1.

Common problems	Analysis criteria (cost factors)
High slopes	◆ High cost of terracing and excavation ◆ Additional costs for building retaining walls ◆ Additional length of pipes to keep low gradient when designing infrastructure and services
Low bearing soils	◆ Larger and deeper foundations ◆ Floating foundations and pilots required ◆ Building retaining surfaces
Damp and poor soils	◆ High cost for removing and excavating ◆ Filling and terracing ◆ Draining and sewerage costs ◆ Rooting ◆ Pumping water
Rocky soils	◆ Excavation costs ◆ High resistance to modify them
Poor drainage	◆ High drainage cost ◆ Excessive deep soil ◆ Deep foundations
Humidity and water filtration	◆ Pilots required ◆ High drainage costs ◆ Floating foundations ◆ Pumping during construction

TABLE 2-1
  Cost analysis criteria for natural terrain variables.

Coding and setting classes for natural variables

Classification methods assign a value scale to each analyzed theme as a function of its cost factor for urban development. The following is a grading method for establishing a range of classes:

❖ High Value (A): Assigned to very attractive land uses. The urban uses defined by this variable are desirable and do not reject the location of other uses or affect the ecological equilibrium of the environment.

❖ Medium Value (M): Assigned to attractive land uses from the standpoint of location and functioning. Land uses defined by this variable affect the location of other uses but do not affect the ecological equilibrium of the site.

❖ Low Value (B): Assigned to areas of unattractive land uses because of more attractive zones or because of doubts about the success of locating such use in this terrain unit. This location, however, does not represent any danger to the ecological equilibrium of the site.

❖ Discarded Value (D): Assigned to areas where urban use must be avoided because it affects the ecological equilibrium of the site.

Assigning A, M, B, or D and a plus or minus indication of desirability for each primary class, we can establish intermediate classes. Table 2-2 shows the grading scheme.

Numerical Value	Class Value	Coding Value
	(A+)	9
8	HIGH (A)	8
	(A-)	7
	(M+)	6
5	MEDIUM (M)	5
	(M-)	4
	(B+)	3
2	LOW (B)	2
	(B-)	1
0	DISCARD (D)	0

TABLE 2-2
Grading scheme for natural variables.

Grading variables and developing conceptual models

Having attribute tables for each terrain unit, we use the Delphi method to grade feasibility or capability. The Delphi method was developed during the 1950s by T. J. Gordon, Olaf Helmer, and Norman Dalkey.

Delphi is an impact assessment methodology that planners and researchers can use to evaluate the feasibility of placing new uses and infrastructures within the settlement. This method requires discussions between the planning team and members of the community to establish weight and evaluation for each variable. The process has two phases: one to weight the variables and another to produce maps and models of the site representing the weight of all variables. Once the model is conceptualized and run in ArcGIS Spatial Analyst, we assign grades to each variable.

Developing feasibility models

For several projects, we used the ModelBuilder tool in ArcGIS Spatial Analyst to run several models showing potential locations for new uses. The grades and weights for each variable were discussed and approved by the community.

For each site, we created three primary models: conservation, recreation, and urbanization.

Each model produces maps showing the existence of conservation, recreation, or urbanization values. This means that for each model, valuable terrain units are those that have the highest grade considering all the variable's weight combinations. Table 2-3 is an example of variable weighting and grading for a conservation model.

Using ModelBuilder to develop a conservation model

With ModelBuilder tools in the ArcGIS Spatial Analyst extension, planners can develop complex models represented as process flow diagrams. Running these models allows planners to create maps that can communicate how the site evaluation is being conducted and show where relationships are established.

ModelBuilder allows planners to do the following:

- ❖ Use property sheets to describe processes. Once a model has been constructed, you can use property sheets to specify how to process the data and display the results.
- ❖ Create a manual or automatic layout. In automatic layout, ModelBuilder will lay out the model diagrams or users can lay out the diagram manually via the manual layout feature.

Variables	Categories	Codes	Weight	Comments
Vegetation	Trees and forest	1	10	Forest type, high trees
	Bushes	2	6	Bushes, low vegetation
	Cultivated land	3	2	Agriculture, pasture
	Water	4	10	Drainage, surface water
	No vegetation	5	2	Barren land
Slopes	0-15%	A	2	Low slopes
	15-30%	B	0	Medium slopes
	> 30%	C	10	High slopes
Hydrography	Intermittent drainage	3	5	Protect and rebuild
	Natural drainage	4	5	Protect
	Lagoons and surface water	5	-99	Discard
	Plain zones	1	1	Plain, flat, low drainage
Geomorphology	Hilly areas, low slopes	2	5	Soft hills, well drained
	Hilly areas, high slopes	3	10	Soft hills, excessively drained
	Sink areas, slide or mass movement	4	10	Badly drained and with possible landslide
Proximity to water courses	Current courses	5	10	Protect
	Badly drained courses	6	5	Depress zones
Combined slope/low vegetation	High slopes	A	10	Protected
	Medium slopes	B	6	
	Forest cover	1	10	Protected

TABLE 2-3
Grading weights (conservation model).

❖ Copy and paste components within a model. You can replicate reoccurring patterns within a model by using the copy and paste commands.

❖ Change properties and then rerun the model. After a model has been run, you can access function property sheets, change the properties specifying how the data is to be processed, and rerun the model.

❖ Change data and then rerun the model. After a model has been run, you can access the data property sheets to select different data themes and then rerun the model.

❖ Compare alternative results. ModelBuilder can be used to create a model with multiple outputs representing alternative evaluation strategies. These outputs can then be compared to assess the differences between alternatives.

❖ Export models into other models. You can use the import and export commands to transfer an entire model, or portion of a model, into another model. This is useful when developing similar models for other sites that have additional variables to consider. In those cases we copy and paste those model portions that analyze the same group of variables.

Conservation model

Figure 2-1 shows the processing flow we used to create a conservation model. The diagram takes into account the weights established in table 2-3. In this case, the conservation model starts reading themes like slopes, vegetation cover, surface drain courses, and geomorphology classes. All of these variables are converted to regular grids with the same cell size, so they become matrices of exactly the same size. For example, we can covert the vegetation coverage to a grid with cells representing 1 × 1 meter. Each one of these cells stores data as a binary code. If the cell stores a zero or blank, the cell contains no vegetation cover. If a number one (1) is stored at that location, the cell represents vegetation cover.

A box is generated indicating the distance from each cell to the nearest cell with vegetation cover or, in other words, with a one (1) stored at the nearest cell. In this stage we get a grid with cells storing distances to the nearest vegetation-covered cells. This matrix is the result of a process shown as a yellow box with the label "Euclidean distance."

Euclidean distance is only one of the many processes that can be selected from the modeling toolbox in ArcGIS Spatial Analyst. In fact, almost any logical process can be defined and created to do what is called map calculation, allowing you to create complex computer models using the data stored as themes in the geodatabase.

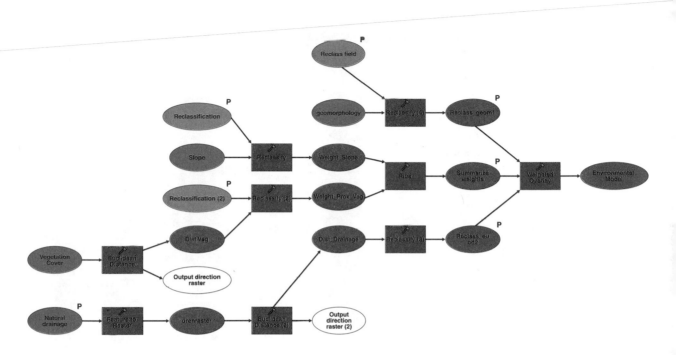

FIGURE 2-1

Process for developing a conservation model using ModelBuilder tools.

Chart by Ramón A. Pérez.

SITE ANALYSIS IN SQUATTER DEVELOPMENTS: A CASE STUDY

We tested our approach to environmental studies in the barrio of Petare Agricultura, one of the most complex barrios in Venezuela. This barrio, which comprises approximately 82 hectares, is located in the east periphery of the capital city of Caracas.

Applying the threshold theory combined with GIS techniques for site analysis, we developed a set of maps and models for Petare. We produced a series of thematic maps using ArcGIS software, then manipulated and combined them to obtain two basic models: conservation and urbanization. A thematic map that gave a clear picture of the complex geography of the site was a combined geomorphology and slope map (figure 2-2).

Using the grading weights in table 2-3 as a basis, we developed a conservation model in ModelBuilder (figure 2-3). In figure 2-3, darker green areas show the highest conservation

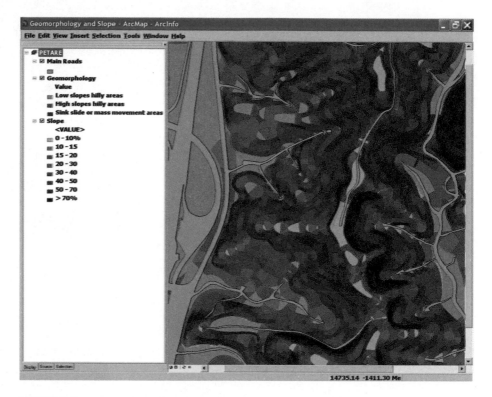

FIGURE 2-2

Geomorphology and slope map of Petare.

Map by Ramón A. Pérez.

values. These high-valued areas should be protected from urban development, but they are entirely occupied by housing development.

ArcGIS allows us to visualize satellite images (figure 2-4) of the site in combination with the resulting conservation model. Combining digital vector themes like topography, vegetation cover, and slope index, all laid over the satellite image, allows us to look closer at the contradictions in squatter developments. For the map in figure 2-5, we used ArcGIS tools to overlay these layers and graduate the transparency of all the layers to create a kind of radiography of the settlement. When we overlaid the conservation model with the shape of each building and made the buildings transparent, we could detect contradictory urban development over areas ranked with a high conservation value.

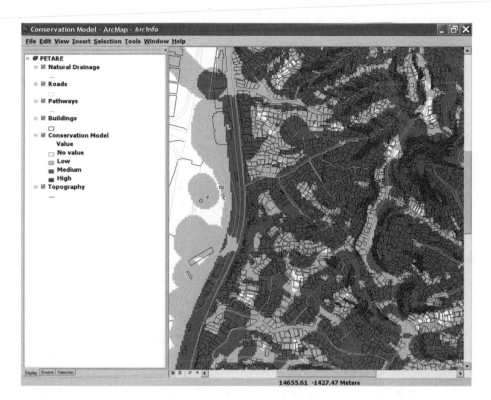

FIGURE 2-3

Conservation model of Petare.

Map by Ramón A. Pérez.

Using GIS, we produced maps by overlaying the conservation model on top of slope classification and enhancing the interpretation by adding some notion of landslide risk due to steep slopes. Adding combinations of other layers such as geomorphology classes, soil types, surface hydrology drainage patterns, and slope classification gave us an even better understanding of the site. Figure 2-6 shows a transparent overlay combination of the conservation model with slopes.

At this point, the proper methodology for doing site analysis with GIS will depend largely on the quality of available data. Generally in developing countries, either some environmental and physiographic data is absent or the available maps showing soil, vegetation types, and geomorphology studies are not reliable or were developed to interpret issues and behavior at other scales.

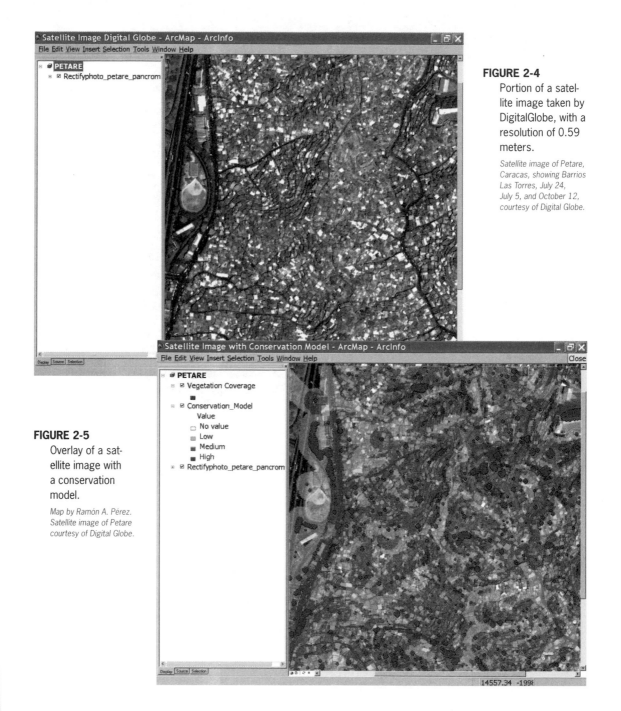

FIGURE 2-4
Portion of a satellite image taken by DigitalGlobe, with a resolution of 0.59 meters.

Satellite image of Petare, Caracas, showing Barrios Las Torres, July 24, July 5, and October 12, courtesy of Digital Globe.

FIGURE 2-5
Overlay of a satellite image with a conservation model.

Map by Ramón A. Pérez. Satellite image of Petare courtesy of Digital Globe.

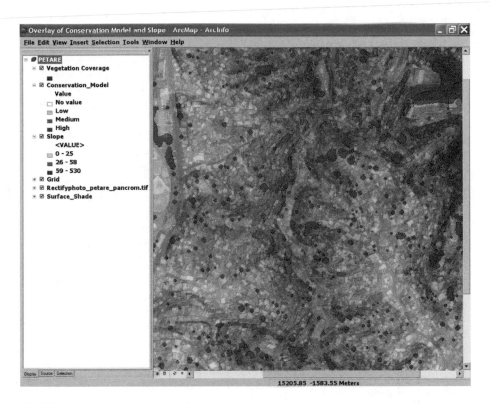

FIGURE 2-6

Transparent overlay combination of the conservation model and slopes.

Map by Ramón A. Pérez. Satellite image of Petare courtesy of Digital Globe.

The lack of data can be mitigated by using interpreted satellite images and collecting some field data. This is what we did in most projects in Venezuela; however, good soil, geology, and vegetation maps should be procured to develop better models and planning results.

If required, the ultimate environmental threshold analysis can be further simplified using Rapid Site Assessment methodology. This methodology allows the planner to evaluate the settlements by using significant variables and combining only those that rapidly explain the urgent issues to resolve. For example, a more explicit map results from turning on the slope layer and making it 50 percent transparent to show the areas of steeper slopes, but also showing unstable geomorphology and soil types to determine locations at higher risk of mass landslides (figure 2-7). The dark pink areas show probable landslide risks.

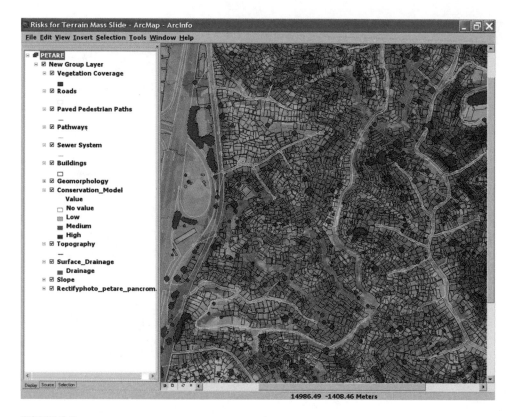

FIGURE 2-7

Risks of mass landslides.

Map by Ramón A. Pérez. Satellite image of Petare courtesy of Digital Globe.

Environmental site evaluation using GIS

In squatter developments, environmental analysis must identify relevant issues that affect community well-being. A combined evaluation of all issues is easier if the proper data is spatially interrelated through GIS. The following steps can guide the site analysis process when using the threshold theory:

Step one: Identify land that should be permanently protected. The developer incorporates areas pre-identified in comprehensive plans or other sources, then performs a detailed site analysis to locate features to be conserved. The developer first identifies all the constrained lands called primary threshold areas and then identifies secondary threshold areas, which comprise noteworthy features of the property typically unprotected under current codes. These areas include mature vegetation cover, surface drainage and stream corridors, hedgerows and individual freestanding trees, pathway corridors, significant structures, scenic viewsheds, and so on.

Some of this data may be available as thematic maps, but many important complementary data items have to be determined in the field—for example, geology and geomorphology data revealing the risk of mass landslides. A site walk is necessary to identify significant site problems, urban landmarks, and other features that should be preserved.

Step two: Combine all physiographic layers with layers defining the primary and secondary thresholds.

Step three: Use ModelBuilder tools in the ArcGIS Spatial Analyst extension to create logical weighting models that summarize and emphasize areas that should be modified to enhance urban quality.

Step four: Create synthesis maps showing the proposed areas of intervention and identify a schedule to build the enhancements. Use GIS to show the phases in time as possible future scenario maps.

The ultimate environment threshold methodology and finally the use of rapid site assessment methodology can help the planner focus only on relevant data. We believe GIS technology can facilitate and accelerate the site analysis process, but if you have no access to GIS software, you can always use transparent sheets of paper to overlay manuscript maps, as Ian McHarg describes (McHarg 1969).

BENEFITS AND LIMITATIONS OF GIS

We recommend GIS for the following reasons:

- ❖ It allows evaluation of the relationship of individual dwellings to the surrounding site from a neighborhood or site perspective.
- ❖ It helps avoid premature decisions that lock the planners into one design before all options have been evaluated.
- ❖ It identifies general site suitability for development, including areas with severe development constraints—where construction costs will be higher—as well as sensitive environmental areas.
- ❖ It documents factors considered in selecting design.
- ❖ It provides a basis for community decisions in a user-friendly visual format.
- ❖ It takes advantage of high-resolution imagery available at both town and regional scales.

❖ It provides access to data such as digital elevation models (DEM). This type of data is available with some satellite imagery.

❖ It allows creation of virtual models of the site (using 3D Analyst tools), which can be seen in 3D, rotated, and overlaid with theme information to discover relations otherwise hidden to the planner's eye.

Keep in mind that GIS does have limitations:

❖ Not all consulting professionals currently use GIS; however, the same process can be performed with large-format, hard-copy maps that can be transparently overlaid.

❖ At this level the information is useful for concept-level planning only.

❖ On-site surveys need to include the following:

  ◆ Soil surveys and geomorphology studies to provide accurate boundaries and land units classifications. This is very important for ultimate threshold analysis.

  ◆ Microbasin edge delineation and vernal pool mapping.

  ◆ Topography (1-meter contours).

  ◆ Vegetation coverage mapping.

  ◆ Other natural, historic, archeological, and scenic resources pertinent to the site analysis.

Developing basic models such as conservation and urbanization is the first step to fully understanding a site's environmental conditions and, therefore, to identifying development constraints. Now that we have an understanding of the natural site, in the following chapter we analyze the urban built environment. In subsequent chapters, we carry out a combined evaluation of environmental and urban built conditions. Analyzing varying combinations of conditions allows us to identify poverty conditions of the site (chapter 4) and also provides a framework for change that will guide the improvement plan (chapter 5).

3

SITE ANALYSIS OF THE URBAN-BUILT

This chapter describes an effective method to analyze the built environment in high-density squatter developments. In traditional site analysis, planners evaluate the urban-built by grading building conditions as good or bad or using categories such as unstable, ruins, and so on. This analysis neglects evaluating the social values hidden behind the physical values of the built environment. In poor urban areas, the urban-built should be evaluated as a container of social values. We need to look deeper within the built environment for evidence of social subdivisions and inhabitants' referential elements.

In a complex urban form, orientation is highly valued by the residents. Physical change can affect the established meaning residents impose on their built environment, and disorientation can lead to confusion and loss in their daily lives. Scenarios for change should be designed within a framework of those social values that have a physical expression, such as elements that define social boundaries or buildings and spaces that serve as community references.

The legibility of the built environment is difficult to discern when the urban form is a compact mass of dwellings. Site analysis must provide answers for questions such as the following: Which and how many social groups are contained within the built? Which built form lodges which social group? What are the boundaries of each group? What are the population and characteristics of each social group? This chapter addresses how planners can get answers to these questions. We will show how we thoroughly analyzed the built environment of a complex squatter development in Venezuela.

A METHOD FOR EVALUATING THE BUILT ENVIRONMENT

To identify the internal physical and social networks contained within the built environment, site analysis must emphasize studies of urban form. We need to establish the capacity of the urban form to support changes without affecting the social network and the inhabitants' systems of orientation. Establishing limits for change becomes fundamental for site analysis. Limits define the maximum changes that the urban form can support without affecting the internal physical and social networks. The basic information needed to establish these limits includes spatial (physical) and nonspatial (social) variables.

The physical network

The physical network constitutes the urban fabric of a settlement because it is the way built elements connect through open space. We usually analyze patterns of connection between individual buildings in typological studies. In massive built forms, where buildings are difficult to individualize, studies should focus on group typologies.

The clustering of dwellings affects our comprehension of the physical and social network. Physical elements that perform a social role, such as pedestrian intersections where groups interact or signs that identify places linked to community history, can be difficult to perceive. Yet identifying these elements is basic to understanding the relationship of social groups to the built environment.

Making maps and visiting the site does not necessarily give a full understanding of boundary lines between social groups. Typological studies provide a better way to understand the physical network.

The social network

Ties between groups constitute the social network, highly appreciated by barrio residents. We have seen residents strongly oppose changes that disrupt or separate them from their kin and friendship groups.

To understand community relations, our first task is to define the boundaries of social groups. Each social group has a spatial domain where they share activities and interests, although, in high-density squatter developments, the physical limits of this domain can be unclear. Our search for ways to define boundaries has shown us that usually streets are not significant for defining boundaries. More than one social group can dwell in a massive built form between existing streets or major pedestrian paths.

Because shared public space is where groups integrate and develop social ties, it becomes a key element to define social boundaries. Within the urban fabric, social groups identify their territory, yet they establish relations through the secondary system of open spaces. When a relevant civic or referential element appears, it becomes a powerful icon for promoting shared feelings of caring for and maintaining the site.

In complex squatter developments, the only way to define community boundaries is through residents' participation. A territorial boundary is knowledge that belongs to the community. Because boundaries are the main social constraints for change, improvement plans must identify and reinforce community boundaries.

PETARE AGRICULTURA: A CASE STUDY

Miles away from the center of the city of Caracas, the settlement of Petare Agricultura appears as a solid built mass placed on the surrounding hillsides. As one comes closer, an

43

anarchic and discontinuous system of vehicular and pedestrian routes appears within the built mass. The visual homogeneity is such that concepts of hierarchy become meaningless. A 3D view generated with ArcScene software shows the homogeneity of the urban form and gives us a sense of confusion, generated by the absence of open space (figure 3-1).

The relation between built and open space shows that 75 percent of the area is densely built and 25 percent is open space, both private and public (figure 3-2).

The social network: Spatial subdivisions and social boundaries

Petare Agricultura contains sixteen barrios, each with several sectors. Sectors represent the spatial unit within which residents develop a strong sense of belonging. This feeling connects to a relatively small public space where social connections occur. The public space is typically a street, a path, or a stairway, which serves as a sector limit. Because these elements constitute a threshold for change, they must be protected as indivisible territory.

FIGURE 3-1

The lower area of the formal city La Urbina adjacent to Petare.

Map by Ramón A. Pérez.

FIGURE 3-2
Complexity of the built form.

Map by Rosario C. Giusti de Pérez and assistants.
Satellite image of Petare courtesy of Digital Globe.

Inside the sector, everybody knows each other and residents can easily identify the boundaries of their sectors and the dwelling units that belong to each of them. The intricacy of the built form and the way buildings within the same block can belong to different sectors give some idea of the difficulties in mapping spatial subdivisions. A fragment of an aerial photograph and a mapped subdivision show the interdependency that can exist between physically belonging to a built group and socially belonging to a community group (figure 3-2).

Improvement projects supported by the Venezuelan government agency FUNDACOMUN use a group of social promoters (promotores sociales) as liaisons with community leaders. The promoters live in the community and organize meetings with the representatives of each barrio. Working with community leaders and residents guarantees that planners will better understand the social network.

FIGURE 3-3

Social subdivisions in Barrios Las Torres, 24 de Julio, 5 de Julio, and 12 de Octobre.

Map by Rosario C. Giusti de Pérez and assistants. Satellite image of Petare, Caracas, showing Barrios Las Torres, July 24, July 5, and October 12, sector subdivision courtesy of Digital Globe.

To develop an improvement plan for Petare Agricultura, the urban planning team and community residents worked together to conduct an exhaustive site and cartographic analysis that established sector boundaries. The community identified 93 sectors within 82 hectares, but spatial subdivisions had not been previously mapped. Dealing with the excessive subdivision of the built environment required accurate spatial delimitations. Using a 1:1000-scale map, we traced sector limits.

To establish relationships between the social space and the built space, we overlaid the sector subdivision with the built form. Overlaying a sector subdivision and an aerial photograph showed the interdependency between both, but social subdivisions and variations in the urban fabric were impossible to detect (figure 3-3).

Mapping social boundaries

The cartography provided by the planning agency could not help us understand the urban form and establish boundaries for small groups. We used GIS to develop a sector map, which showed each sector was a social unit. Using a numerical and alphabetical code, we identified barrios with letters and sectors with numbers. Numerical order was established starting north, moving west toward the left, and increasing sequentially.

Subdivisions showed that some barrio sectors were located outside the boundaries of the urban design unit of Petare Agricultura. We redefined boundaries to include these additional sectors. With definite limits, we calculated area, number of dwellings and families, population densities, and building densities per sector (figure 3-4).

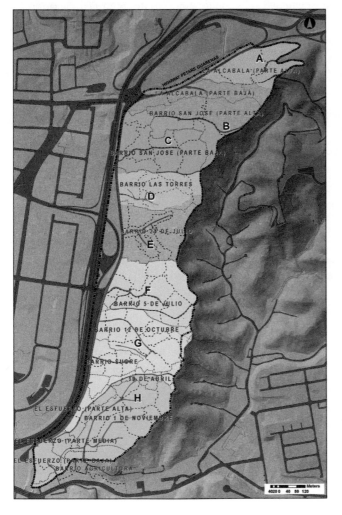

NEIGHBORHOOD (BARRIO) NAME	NUMBER OF SECTORS
LA ALCABALA (PARTE BAJA)	4
LA ALCABALA (PARTE ALTA)	2
SAN JOSÉ (PARTE BAJA)	5
SAN JOSÉ (PARTE ALTA)	9
CALLEJON TORRES	6
24 DE JULIO	8
12 DE OCTUBRE (*)	9
5 DE JULIO	17
SUCRE	7
1 DE NOVIEMBRE	7
VISTA ALEGRE	1
19 DE ABRIL (*)	8
EL ESFUERZO (PARTE ALTA)	3
EL ESFUERZO (PARTE MEDIA)	2
EL ESFUERZO (PARTE BAJA)	2
AGRICULTURA (*)	3

(*) INCLUDES SECTORS BELONGING TO NEIGHBORHOODS LOCATED OUTSIDE THE STUDY AREA.

FIGURE 3-4

Population chart with barrio and sector subdivisions.

Map by Rosario C. Giusti de Pérez and assistants.

Population studies

To begin studying population in squatter developments, we need to relate data collection to social units. In the Venezuelan General XII Census for population and dwellings conducted in 2001, the smallest unit of spatial data is the census tract, or block; however, it is a statistical unit and not a social unit. For each census tract, the census report provides information about the number of dwellings and household size.

Since census tracts are continuous and spatially exceed the sectors (social units), our first step is to search for a territorial unit where blocks could be physically contained. Because hydrographic basins have a clear spatial definition that avoids splitting of census tracts, we can use basins to estimate the total population by adding the population of all contained census tracts.

The second task is to determine population per sector and estimate the number of dwellings for each community subdivision. For settlements where dwellings pile up on top of each other, we need three-dimensional data to identify how many dwellings are under each roof. Available maps and aerial photographs provide only two-dimensional data. To overcome this problem, we established a dwellings-per-roof index, using the total number of dwellings per basin and the total number of roofs. In Petare, where ninety-three sectors are located within eight hydrographic basins, we used this approach to estimate the population per sector. Census information gave us the number of tracts and therefore the number of dwellings per basin.

Using ArcGIS tools to intersect the basin areas with the roofs that fell within them, we obtained the number of roofs located in each basin (figure 3-5 shows rooftops in the central area of Petare). To obtain the dwellings-per-roof index, we divided the number of dwellings (provided by the census) by the number of roofs per basin. Figure 3-6 shows basin divisions and the population per basin.

Having the dwellings-per-roof index, we can estimate the population for each social unit or sector. Using GIS tools, we counted the number of roofs per sector and multiplied this number by the dwellings-per-roof index. With the household size for each basin, we obtained the population per sector. Having areas and their populations, we estimated residential densities. The study of densities showed that the average density for the entire urban design unit of Petare Agricultura was 697 inhabitants per hectare, one of the highest in metropolitan Caracas.

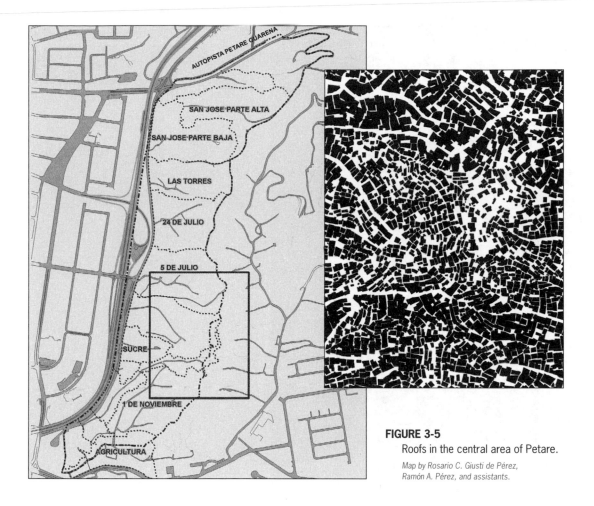

FIGURE 3-5
Roofs in the central area of Petare.

*Map by Rosario C. Giusti de Pérez,
Ramón A. Pérez, and assistants.*

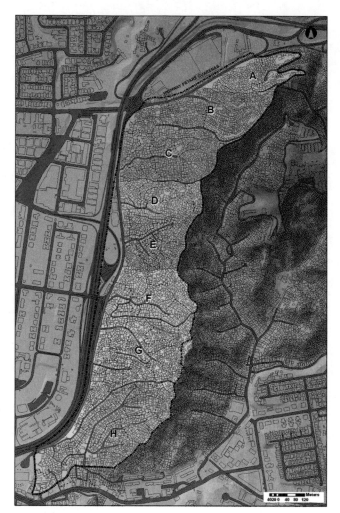

NUMBER OF DWELLINGS PER BASIN.					
BASIN CODE	DWELLINGS 2001	PERSONS/ DWELLING	POPULATION	NO. OF ROOFS	INDEX DWELLING/ ROOF
A	454	5,36	2.431	412	1,1
B	1.247	5,93	7.392	1.247	1,35
C	1.489	5.56	8.276	1.489	1,58
D	577	5,97	3.445	458	1,26
E	657	5,33	3.498	617	1,06
F	1.257	5,49	6.899	678	1,85
G	2.036	5,24	10.673	1.058	1,92
H	2.121	5,46	11.586	1.129	1,88
TOTAL	9.837	5,51	54.202	7.088	---------

FIGURE 3-6

Basin divisions and the population per basin.

Map by Rosario C. Giusti de Pérez and assistants.

Sectors and basic management units (condominiums)

Our analysis showed great variations between population size and area per sector. Sectors with more than one thousand inhabitants will require additional subdivisions to obtain manageable units. Whenever sectors require subdivisions, we consult with the community to get their approval of our definition of limits. We called the basic management unit "condominium." Small sectors can be condominiums and large sectors can house more than one condominium. The basis for defining condominiums is knowing the number of families and the urban form of the area.

It is important to point out that condominium definition is fundamental to identifying the public space where social interaction takes place. The dimensions of this space allow community control and maintenance. Condominiums also represent a way to develop and consolidate strong community ties. We will discuss condominiums in more detail in chapter 7.

THE PHYSICAL NETWORK

In Petare Agricultura, residential use occupies approximately 70 percent of the area. Commercial use occurs at ground level in the periphery around sectors of the Petare Guarenas highway. Inside the settlement, health and educational services are located along access roads. Only in very few cases do we find nonresidential uses, such as small churches or plazas, inside the residential fabric.

The initial step for analyzing the urban fabric is to define spatial groups. Having a sector definition, we studied the different ways building units cluster to define groups. Analyses related to physical change include identifying possibilities where we can substitute old buildings with new ones and find possibilities to increase the height of existing buildings. Improvement proposals based on building substitution depend on built group typologies; however, height increase depends on the possibility of adding floors. Building substitution is a planned process, but height increase is a natural process of change controlled through development rules.

Built group typologies

To define group typologies, we analyzed the way dwelling units cluster and constitute groups. In some cases, clustering can be independent from the open space system. Inside the settlement where land occupation follows topography, building disposition is independent of roads and paths.

We organized and defined group typologies using the road network. For example, where roads follow urban occupation, the dwellings also follow the alignment of the roads. Where urban occupation does not follow road alignment, we find block-type clusters of buildings, with dwellings piling up in an indivisible mass. These block types adjust to topography and are typical in the interior areas of Petare. Some areas have a combination of buildings, which may or may not be aligned with roads or paths. In network dead ends, groups of buildings combine both road alignment and block-type clustering.

Built types

The predominant typology is the block. A block is a group typology and differs from the block that represents a census tract. The latter can group dwellings of different types, such as detached, twin units, rows, and so forth; however, a block typology is a clustering of similar dwelling units.

Individual units are scarce and spread over the area. We used two block typologies: linear and multidirectional. Linear blocks are row attachments of different length. Twin units are a special category in the row typology. Multidirectional blocks are clusters of dwellings irregularly attached in a mountain-type mass that can reach up to four floors. Two types of multidirectional blocks exist: compact or branched.

Common building elements shared by a number of dwellings make block typologies difficult to change. Block clusters are like a castle made of cards, where a precarious equilibrium depends on the interrelated distribution of structural forces. Removing a dwelling unit from a compact block can collapse the whole. Dwellings located in the periphery of blocks are easier to modify or eliminate without affecting the whole. Branched blocks, for example, can lose end dwellings without affecting the whole. Figure 3-7 shows building typologies.

Building dimensions

The size of a building is usually considered important when defining typologies. To classify building sizes, we conducted a cartographic review of the roof size. Buildings having up to 80 square meters were classified as small, between 81 and 150 square meters as medium, and over 150 square meters as large. We mapped these categories and compared that map with a map of building typologies (figure 3-8).

The comparison showed that clustering and attachment are independent from building size. The lack of connection between dimension and clustering reveals the irrelevance of building size when classifying built groups. Size becomes important when dwelling units are relocated, since the value of each square meter has to be paid to the owner of the relocated building unit.

Building heights

Typologies such as detached dwellings or single-story dwellings located in the periphery of compact clusters of units can increase in height. Possibilities for increasing height, even if slightly, means additional population can be lodged.

In Petare, where vacant land is scarce and growth cannot be totally stopped, vertical growth promises to increase in the coming years. The structural capacity of the built to accept

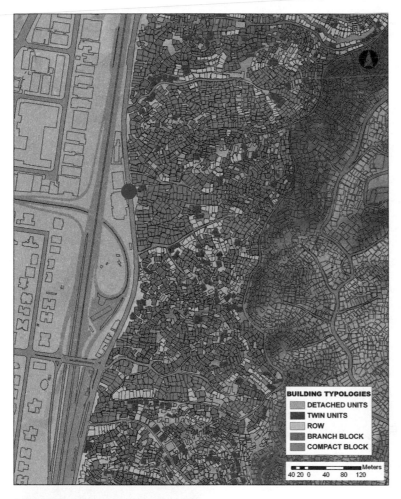

BUILDING TYPOLOGIES
- DETACHED UNITS
- TWIN UNITS
- ROW
- BRANCH BLOCK
- COMPACT BLOCK

Meters
40 20 0   40   80   120

FIGURE 3-7
Building typologies.

*Map and photo by Rosario C. Giusti de Pérez
and assistants.*

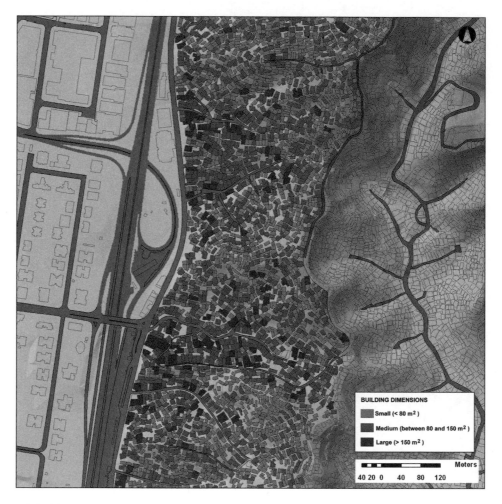

FIGURE 3-8
Building dimensions.

Map by Rosario C. Giusti de Pérez and assistants.

additional floors becomes a limitation for vertical growth; nonetheless, height increase will not change the group typology. Using ArcGIS software, we generated a map that displayed building heights (figure 3-9), which helped us see which areas held major or minor possibilities for future vertical growth.

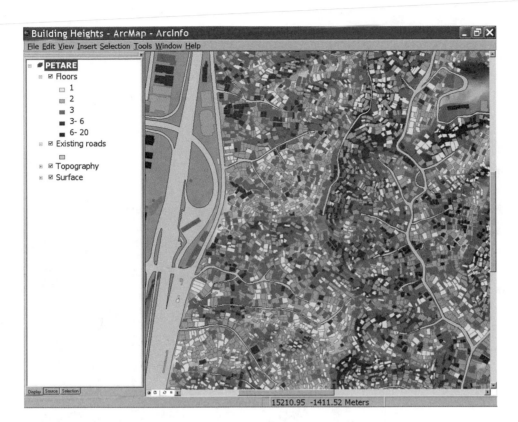

FIGURE 3-9
  Building heights.

  Map by Rosario C. Giusti de Pérez and assistants.

The open space system

Open space in Petare is a system of access roads disconnected from each other, combined with a continuous and vast system of pedestrian paths. Existing roads are narrow and steep. Circulation is difficult for standard vehicles and most routes allow only one-way traffic. Additionally, in some sections of the road, abandoned vehicles interfere with circulation.

The western periphery of the urban design unit is a highway, Autopista Petare Guarenas, running north–south. An access road in the south central area climbs the hill to the upper sectors and becomes the eastern peripheral road, which also runs north-south. Other than these two roads, north–south vehicular connections are nonexistent. Two independent secondary road systems exist: one in the north central area and one in the south. The north central area is conformed by a series of dead-end roads that penetrate from the western highway or from the eastern peripheral road. The southern area has its own road system that enters the urban design unit (UDU) from the highway. The southern area has no physical border toward the east.

The pedestrian routes comprise a dense, complex system of narrow stairs and pathways (figure 3-10). Modification seems difficult, but improving stairs and pathways is possible. Understanding how the open space weaves between buildings and identifying possible continuities require a separate analysis.

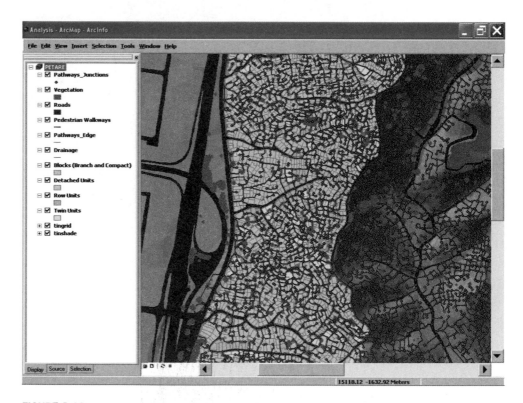

FIGURE 3-10

Characteristics of the pedestrian web.

Map by Rosario C. Giusti de Pérez and assistants.

The urban structure

The homogeneity of the urban fabric and the discontinuous open space system generate a confused urban structure. With GIS we presented the distribution of buildings and open space, and with analysis we detected patterns of development. The pattern of the development showed the following spatial characteristics (figure 3-11):

❖ In general, the sixteen barrios are not connected.

❖ Except for the southern area, urban occupation has developed in an east–west direction moving toward connections to the eastern peripheral road.

❖ Barrios located in the south that are disconnected from the rest of the area have a different occupation imposed by their secondary system of access roads.

❖ Public or civic activities are scarce.

❖ The quality and quantity of open space is low.

❖ The pedestrian system is a barrier for improving open space and tracing pipelines.

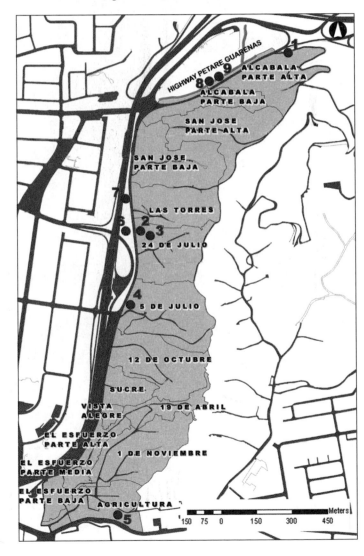

FIGURE 3-11

Spatial characteristics of the urban structure.

Map by Rosario C. Giusti de Pérez and assistants.

FIGURE 3-11 *(cont.)*
Spatial characteristics of
the urban structure.

*Photos by Rosario C. Giusti de Pérez
and assistants.*

FIGURE 3-11 *(cont.)*
Spatial characteristics of
the urban structure.

*Photos by Rosario C. Giusti de Pérez
and assistants.*

FIGURE 3-11 *(cont.)*
Spatial characteristics of
the urban structure.

*Photos by Rosario C. Giusti de Pérez
and assistants.*

A PRELIMINARY SCENARIO FOR CHANGE

A complete understanding of the built environment helps planners visualize scenarios for improvement. Preserving the social boundaries is the basis for developing preliminary physical design scenarios; however, these scenarios have to encompass the constraints and opportunities of the geographic characteristics of the site. A sustainable scenario for development must fit building and social needs within the conditions dictated by the geography of the site.

Improvement projects that acknowledge and appreciate the built as a container of social values can be developed after planners do the following:

❖ Identify the social subdivisions through dialogues with community residents who know the social boundaries.

❖ Understand the physical network, identifying the relevant elements appreciated by community residents.

❖ Compare the physical and social network to establish a spatial correspondence.

❖ Study urban form to identify typologies and hidden functional orders.

❖ Analyze the urban fabric and open space system to propose a rational organization of the settlement supported in the existing urban order.

With GIS, we could translate data about the urban-built that came from different sources (e.g., CAD, DGN, MIF, and DXF files, rasters, images, dBase tables) into a single geographical format. To import all the available spatial and nonspatial data, we used ArcCatalog and ArcToolbox. Because we could overlay various layers related to building characteristics and query attributes, we could identify where building heights could increase or where dwellings could be replaced or substituted. GIS will not solve the problems of poverty, but it will provide the analysis tools to help us identify where and when change must happen, which ultimately helps us obtain better results when planning urban development.

Mapping poverty as a complementary task will help planners rationally allocate resources available for upgrading programs. When grades of poverty are identified, resources can be directed to more deprived areas. The next chapter discusses an approach to poverty mapping.

4

POVERTY MAPPING

Improving quality of life for residents is the main goal of any improvement project. Quality-of-life indicators reflect a community's well-being. Because poverty indicators also measure a community's collective well-being, they are alternative ways of expressing quality of life.

Prioritizing areas for improvement are typical aspects of urban planning projects. Traditional planning establishes priorities based on a diagnosis of the physical conditions of the settlement. Such planning detects the need for infrastructure—where residential areas can be renewed and where roads and urban services can be improved—and generally approaches these tasks individually.

Measuring and mapping poverty has become the best way to establish priorities and assign resources; however, because of complexity, most poverty studies target only particular aspects of urban poverty. In poor areas, the places needing the most improvement—along with the people who live in these places—should be determined using an integrated approach, where poverty indexes embrace a wide variety of spatial and nonspatial variables. The era of the predominance of socioeconomic indicators serving as the main source for measuring poverty is ending. A newer, integrated vision of poverty, where spatial and nonspatial components are equally weighed and measured, is emerging.

URBAN POVERTY

According to the World Bank, one-third of the people in developing countries who live in cities live in squatter settlements (see http://web.worldbank.org). Projections for increases in the urban population have shifted traditional poverty analysis focusing on rural areas toward focusing on cities. The increase of urban poor associated with city growth is now a priority for city planners.

The increase in the dimension and number of squatter developments in urban areas affects a city's ability to function as a unified unit, creating a parallel city, also called an informal city, which is a conurbation of barrios forming a peripheral ring of poverty around the city. Upgrading the poverty conditions of this urban ring will balance the quality of life in both the formal city and the informal city. To allocate resources for upgrading programs in a balanced way, we need to identify grades of poverty.

SPATIAL AND NONSPATIAL POVERTY

Even when the poor increase their incomes, and therefore their individual quality of life, their surrounding urban space continues to be deprived. Poverty conditions in physical space have to be measured in terms of their arrangement and conditioning. Are buildings deteriorated? Do they need to be painted? Is the open space well maintained? Does it have enough lighting? Does the open space have any trees? Is there enough open space to allow neighbors to meet each other? Measuring the poverty conditions of urban space to identify what has to be done to improve quality of life is important for the well-being of communities.

We can combine socioeconomic conditions, measured as nonphysical (or nonspatial) components, with urban poverty, measured in physical or spatial components. Further, some nonphysical components, such as the network of social and community relationships, are spatially dependant. When planners measure nonspatial urban poverty, they need to analyze and visualize the physical habitat. This approach guides our analysis and mapping of spatial poverty. Having an accurate picture of the urban space allows us to develop upgrading proposals that reinforce the social network contained within the built environment.

Indicators for spatial poverty

An appropriate selection of spatial indicators provides a better and more sustainable approach for upgrading deprived areas. Because of their physical expression, spatial poverty indicators can be seen and understood by everyone. Poverty components may be hidden when the urban occupation occurs in flatlands, but can become an aggressive visual manifestation when they occur on hillsides above valleys. These different expressions involve different complexities, and high-density squatter developments occupying hillside areas are the most complex of all.

The various dimensions of spatial poverty can be visible or invisible. Some poverty indicators are clearly visible, such as dilapidated housing, and others, such as accessibility or the absence of sewers, are invisible. We used GIS to develop a model to measure quality of life. Combining visible and invisible spatial poverty indicators gives us a complete picture of the poverty of the settlement. Grades of poverty are expressed as differences in quality of life.

A MODEL FOR MEASURING QUALITY OF LIFE

To measure quality of life, we developed two parallel measuring processes, one based on visible spatial indicators and the other on invisible ones. Visible indicators include dwellings built with discarded or waste materials, residual public space frequently used for waste disposal, environmental problems such as landslides, and lack of vegetation.

Invisible indicators include accessibility to urban facilities, public transportation, and infrastructure networks. The distance residents travel to access facilities usually located in the formal city is one of the primary invisible indicators of poverty. Access difficulties increase urban poverty because they decrease quality of life.

Manifestations of spatial poverty

Among the multiple manifestations of spatial poverty, some are more significant than others, depending on the settlement's characteristics. The following components reflect poverty conditions in a squatter development around the world:

1. Low availability and quality of public space
2. Precarious conditions of the built environment
3. Difficult and adverse circulating conditions within the settlement
4. Lack of access to public transportation and surrounding facilities of the formal city
5. Lack of access to urban infrastructure

Components 1 and 2 are visible and 3, 4, and 5 are invisible. Connecting these components gives us an integrated view of urban poverty that can be translated into grades of quality of life. Figure 4-1 shows typical manifestations of spatial poverty in high-density squatter developments.

MEASURING VISIBLE POVERTY

To accurately measure visible poverty, we analyze each component separately. For example, looking at a combination of a dwelling's appearance and its surrounding exterior space provides a visible picture of poverty. Combining all components that constitute the urban scene is the best expression of visible poverty.

Availability and quality of public space

In high-density squatter developments, open public space usually consists of only 5 to 10 percent of the available land. In contrast, 30 percent of the space in a formal city is public. The relationship between open space and total urban occupation is, by itself, a poverty indicator. The quality of public space helps determine whether the index of poverty is major or minor.

Types of access to buildings provide differences in the quality of urban space. Semiprivate space gives richness to public space. Because a wider open space allows natural lighting to break through and the visibility provides more security, it is rated as higher quality. Very

FIGURE 4-1
Manifestations of poverty
in squatter developments.

*Photos by Rosario C. Giusti
de Pérez and assistants.*

narrow public spaces can produce a sense of excessive enclosure and dark areas, diminishing security and therefore quality of life.

Conditions of the built environment

Poverty conditions of the built environment can be graded by identifying the conditions of each dwelling or the restrictions for change of groups of dwellings. Improving individual dwellings is always a possibility, yet when dwellings cluster and, as a consequence, share structural elements such as slabs and columns, restrictions for change can be difficult and expensive.

MEASURING INVISIBLE POVERTY

A common measure of invisible poverty is the time that barrio residents spend accessing facilities located in the formal city. Generally, health care, education, and transportation facilities in the formal city do not have the capacity to absorb the demand of additional population, which aggravates the problems of the poor.

Access to employment opportunities also relates to access to the surrounding city. When large employment centers are located far away from the settlement, the often excessive time spent trying to reach these centers becomes a measurement of life quality and, therefore, of poverty conditions.

Circulating conditions

When illegal occupation occurs on steep slopes, people use different modes of transportation to move, but the movement itself is arduous. The concentration of dwellings on such hillsides generates an irregular pattern of circulation—via vehicles, walking, or other means. Possibilities for vehicular access are limited to the periphery of the settlement and access to most residential areas is limited to pedestrians. Sometimes access becomes severe and inhabitants have to climb an equivalent of up to forty floors to reach their dwelling. Downhill travel to surrounding facilities requires less physical effort, but inhabitants are aware of the strenuous uphill return. Pedestrian routes that require intense physical effort increase the condition of poverty.

Access to public transportation, the formal city, and urban infrastructure

To measure invisible poverty, we analyze each of the components related to access to urban facilities within the settlement and from the settlement to the surrounding formal city.

When measuring accessibility, it is important to identify what we are accessing. When we deal with distance to urban services, surrounding facilities, or employment centers, it's best to measure walking distance. Access to public transportation, such as distances to bus stops and roads, is measured in meters or feet.

We establish poverty indexes to measure access to infrastructure networks such as water supply, sewers, waste facilities, and so on. Poverty is usually measured as a lack of these facilities; however, it can also be measured by giving weight to constraints for access such as distances and terrain barriers. Having access to none, one, two, or all of these public services or networks can establish differences in poverty levels and therefore in quality of life.

MAPPING POVERTY

Using visible and invisible indicators, we mapped poverty for two settlements: Petare and Los Claveles. Petare was part of a five-year World Bank program for upgrading squatter developments in Caracas, even though national planning agencies would continue implementing the plan for an additional five years. Plans for Los Claveles were sponsored by the municipal council of the state of Vargas, where the settlement is located.

Los Claveles and Petare are similar developments, yet their complexities differ. Both are located in the surrounding hillsides of a major city and both suffer from a pronounced lack of public facilities and accessibility. Both have common environmental problems typical of irregular topography. Petare has higher densities and nonexistent vacant land. In Los Claveles, a 1999 landslide worsened environmental problems, leaving several ruined areas.

The information available about each settlement was different. For Los Claveles, we based our analysis on a physical census carried out for the whole settlement. In Petare, we used cartographic information, aerial photographs, visits to the site, and population surveys.

To map poverty, we analyze each component separately and combine them in a synthesis map. Components and combinations depend on the available information and the type of settlement.

To map visible poverty, we used information about the public space and conditions of the built environment. A combination of these two components gives us a picture of the poverty of the urban scene and allows us to map visible poverty.

To map invisible poverty, we used information about the difficult circulating conditions within the settlement, the access to public transportation, existing inner facilities, surrounding public services of the formal city, and access to urban infrastructure.

POVERTY OF THE BUILT ENVIRONMENT

To establish grades of poverty in Los Claveles, we used the building conditions of roofs and walls provided by the census. Concrete roofs combined with brick and block walls represent good building conditions. Roofs and walls made of wood, zinc, and asbestos are considered very poor building conditions. Different combinations of materials produce in-between grades. The resulting poverty map of the built environment per dwelling is shown in figure 4-2.

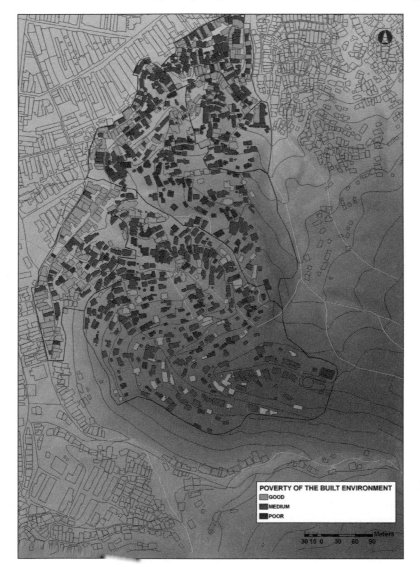

POVERTY OF THE BUILT ENVIRONMENT
GOOD
MEDIUM
POOR

30 15 0   30   60   90   Meters

FIGURE 4-2
Poverty of the built environment per dwelling in Los Claveles.

Map by Rosario C. Giusti de Pérez and assistants.

Because Petare has a homogeneous, clustered appearance, individual building conditions are irrelevant for defining grades of poverty. Differences in the quality of dwellings depend on their possibilities for being improved. Dwellings that belong to a compact group have low improvement possibilities and dwellings adjacent to roads have higher possibilities. Poverty of the built is associated with restrictions for improvement; therefore, we used group typologies defined in chapter 3 as poverty indicators (figure 4-3). We identified three categories: medium poor for individual dwellings and linear blocks, poor for multidirectional branched blocks, and very poor for compact blocks. Dwellings adjacent to roads are generally in better condition, so they are classified as medium poor.

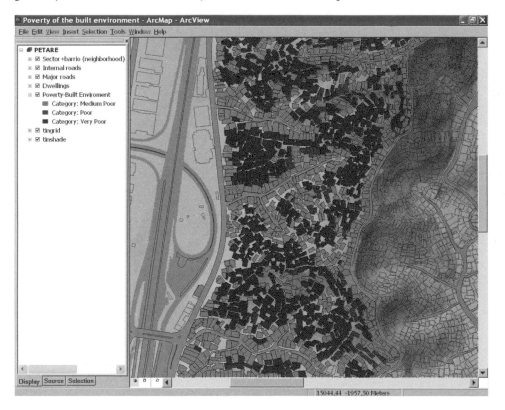

FIGURE 4-3

Poverty of the built environment in Petare.

Map by Rosario C. Giusti de Pérez and assistants.

Poverty of public space

To identify the poverty of public space, we used the census form for Los Claveles. In Petare we compared the index of open space to total urban occupation to define grades of poverty. The predominant homogeneity of the indicator made grading poverty irrelevant.

To establish the poverty of public space in Los Claveles (figure 4-4), we weighed two variables from the census form: type of access to the dwellings and existence of an intermediate space between public space and the entrance door to a dwelling. Access can be through a street, a path, or a stair and the in-between space can be a front garden or a porch. The existence of an intermediate space defines higher quality.

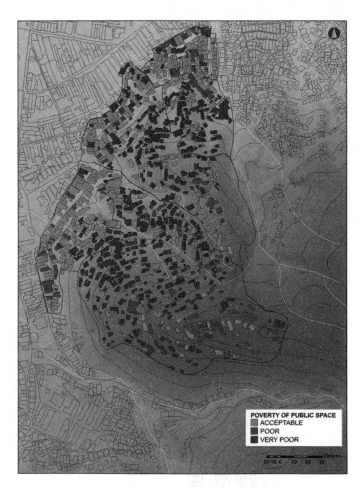

POVERTY OF PUBLIC SPACE
ACCEPTABLE
POOR
VERY POOR

30 15 0   30   60   90
Meters

FIGURE 4-4

Poverty of the public space in Los Claveles.

Map by Rosario C. Giusti de Pérez and assistants.

Poverty of the internal circulating system

Differences in the internal functioning of Los Claveles and Petare require that we use different poverty measurements. Petare has a homogeneous internal circulation system that affects the entire settlement except for the low peripheral areas. We perceived an increase in poverty conditions because of how long it took pedestrians to travel their daily routes.

Los Claveles has no internal facilities; therefore, residents depend completely on facilities located in the surrounding city. The lack of internal roads and the difficult pedestrian routes result in a general lack of accessibility to and from Los Claveles (figure 4-5). The lower areas

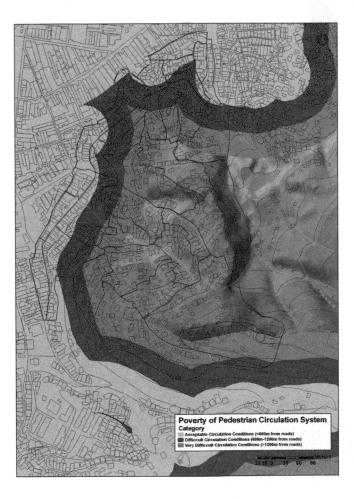

Poverty of Pedestrian Circulation System
Category
Acceptable Circulation Conditions (<600m from roads)
Difficult Circulation Conditions (600m-1200m from roads)
Very Difficult Circulation Conditions (>1200m from roads)

FIGURE 4-5

Poverty conditions in Los Claveles measured in circulation difficulties.

Map by Rosario C. Giusti de Pérez and assistants.

73

have good access, but above 600 meters, the circulation system is irregular and steep. After 1,200 meters, the slopes become even steeper and access is extremely difficult.

Petare has very steep slopes combined with an intricate pedestrian system, making a walking journey slow and difficult. We intersected the Petare slope map with the pedestrian system and classified circulation difficulties for each path. The difficulties of internal pedestrian circulation are measured in expected walking speed from each dwelling to urban services located in the surrounding city (figure 4-6).

To visualize the pedestrian routes available for residents to access urban facilities, we built a network of pedestrian paths across each urban settlement. Squatter developments do not

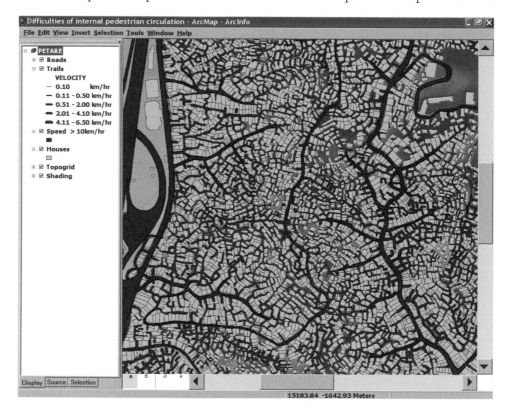

FIGURE 4-6

Difficulties of internal pedestrian circulation in Petare.

Map by Ramón A. Pérez.

have paved pathways and trails, so digitizing this network by normal means is not possible. To define the pedestrian network, we created the following procedure:

1. We converted the settlement map usually provided by the public agency in vector CAD format into a raster format. This allowed us to visualize the dwellings in white and the open spaces in black. Wider and darker lines are less difficult paths for pedestrian circulation.

2. Using ArcScan for ArcGIS, we vectorized the binary raster file to define all possible pedestrian paths. If we had a satellite image or an orthophotograph of the settlement, we could also create this binary raster and use ArcScan for vectorizing walking trails.

Accessibility to facilities and public transportation (poverty index)

In Petare, where accessibility problems affect large numbers of people, we made additional poverty measurements. We defined a poverty index by developing a combined analysis of the speed of internal circulation and access to urban facilities and public transportation. Using the ArcView Network Analyst extension, we estimated the distance and time from each dwelling to basic urban facilities (see figure 4-7) using the following procedure:

1. We combined the previously generated vectors of the pedestrian network with the lines and arcs representing the city streets network. With this combination we could see ways to connect the pedestrian pathways with the formal city transportation network.

2. We converted this combined vector network into a topologically functional network so we could calculate and define the shortest routes to access public services.

3. We assigned grades of impedance to the pedestrian network. Impedance is associated with steep slopes, walking upward or downward, the existence or lack of paved walkways, stairs, bridges, and other facilities like plazas.

Intersecting surface-walking speed data (figure 4-7) with dwellings, we defined the difficulties of accessing urban services from each dwelling (figure 4-8). Larger symbols identify higher velocities, which mean higher accessibility ratings for pedestrian circulation.

Building the poverty index (general accessibility)

In Petare, building an adequate poverty index requires combining elements that measure the multiple variables affected by a difficult access. To define this index, we used accessibility data related to the difficulties of the internal circulation system and a dwelling accessibility index (figure 4-9).

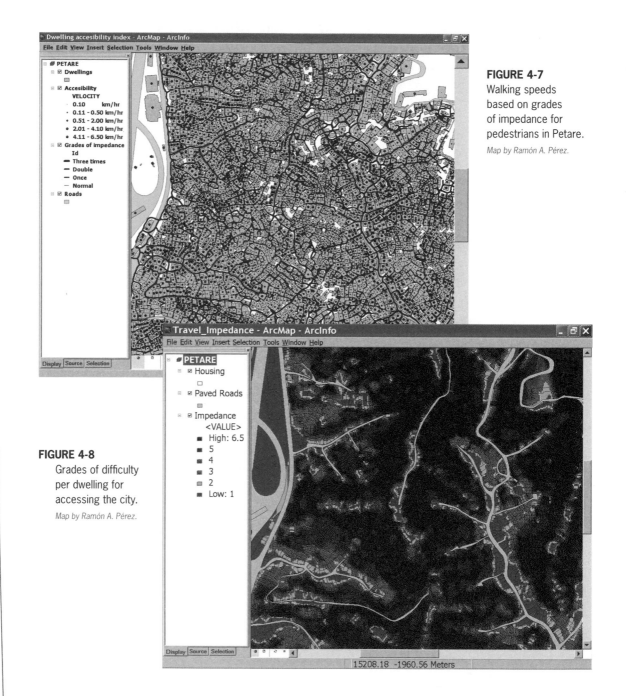

FIGURE 4-7
Walking speeds
based on grades
of impedance for
pedestrians in Petare.

Map by Ramón A. Pérez.

FIGURE 4-8
Grades of difficulty
per dwelling for
accessing the city.

Map by Ramón A. Pérez.

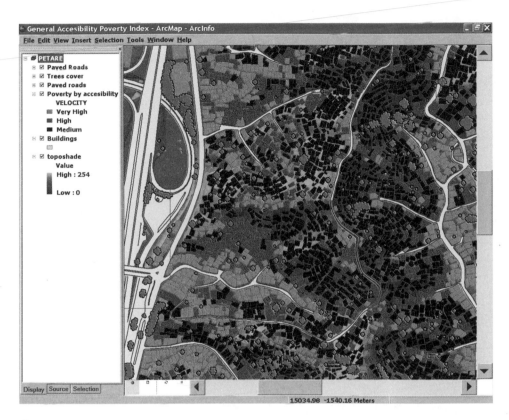

FIGURE 4-9

General accessibility poverty index for Petare.

Map by Ramón A. Pérez.

VISIBLE POVERTY MAPS

Buildings and open space are the main components of the urban scene; therefore, we combined poverty of the built environment and poverty of public space to develop maps showing visible poverty. These maps illustrate the poverty of the urban scene in each settlement.

For Los Claveles we combined poverty maps of the built environment and public space to obtain three categories of visible poverty: acceptable, poor, and very poor (figure 4-10). Since public space conditions in Petare didn't make a difference, we could directly translate poverty of the built environment (figure 4-3) into a visible poverty map.

VISIBLE POVERTY (URBAN SCENE PER AREA)
CATEGORY
LOW POVERTY
MEDIUM POVERTY
HIGH POVERTY

Meters
30 15 0   30   60   90

FIGURE 4-10
Visible poverty for Los Claveles.

Map by Rosario C. Giusti de Pérez and assistants.

INVISIBLE POVERTY MAPS

To map invisible poverty, we analyzed the same type of information we used for visible poverty: a physical census for Los Claveles and statistical information and aerial photographs for Petare. For each settlement, we used different poverty indicators; however, for both, we translated significant poverty indexes directly into invisible poverty categories.

To obtain an invisible poverty map for Los Claveles, we translated categories from the internal circulation system poverty map (figure 4-5) to invisible poverty categories. For Petare, we also translated categories from the map showing difficulties for accessing any type of urban services and infrastructure (figure 4-9) into poverty categories. In both cases, we assigned three poverty categories: medium, high, and very high.

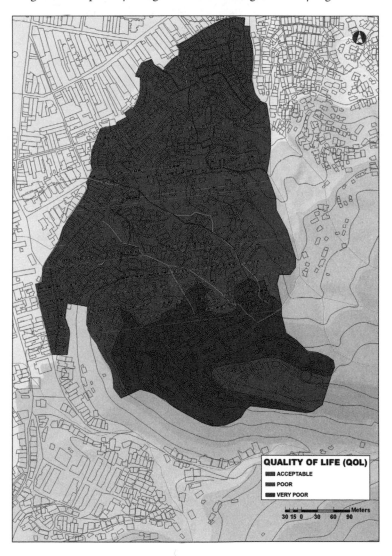

QUALITY OF LIFE (QOL)
■ ACCEPTABLE
■ POOR
■ VERY POOR

FIGURE 4-11
Quality of life in Los Claveles.

Map by Rosario C. Giusti de Pérez and assistants.

FIGURE 4-12

Quality of life in Petare.

Map by Ramón A. Pérez.

GRADES OF POVERTY AND QUALITY OF LIFE

To obtain grades of poverty and quality of life, we combined visible and invisible poverty maps. For Los Claveles, we identified three categories: acceptable, poor, and very poor (figure 4-11). For Petare we identified four categories: acceptable, medium, poor, and very poor (figure 4-12).

Grading quality of life allows us to propose urban intervention policies per sector. In the short run, we can improve poor grades and change extreme poverty to acceptable. This can make crucial differences in residents' quality of life.

When we evaluate the built environment to establish a framework for change, poverty maps provide a useful guide to help us identify areas requiring major planning emphasis. Poverty maps become fundamental when planners are timing the stages of plan implementation. Usually the very poor areas are taken care of during initial stages of the plan execution.

In the following chapter, we evaluate the built environment to establish where and how to make changes that increase quality of life.

5

URBAN PLANNING FOR SQUATTER DEVELOPMENTS

Usually a major removal or renewal of the existing settlement is the first idea considered when planning improvements for squatter developments. Practically speaking, however, any available funds will probably not be sufficient to implement major changes. Large areas of cities in developing countries demand improvement, and the existing funds usually have to be distributed across several settlements. What should be improved and how much? What is feasible and what is not? To answer these questions, we need a complete formal and functional understanding of each settlement.

Meetings with community groups at the beginning of the planning process are essential. Proposals for change need to balance environmental constraints, which planners are obligated to protect, with community demands to preserve buildings or continue activities that have negative impacts. To be sustainable, interventions must fit within a framework consistent with environmental and social values.

A combined evaluation of the environment and the urban-built conditions that we described in chapters 2, 3, and 4 provides the framework for change that guides the improvement plan. The dual purpose of spatial change is to improve quality of life and provide additional facilities required by population growth. In this chapter we use that combined evaluation to design urban development proposals that are feasible and sustainable. We will describe how we developed projects for Petare and Los Claveles, the two barrios for which we developed poverty maps in chapter 4.

FEASIBILITY OF INTERVENTIONS OF THE BUILT

Whether interventions are feasible depends on the social and physical characteristics of the settlements. The social boundaries (social network) and the physical order guide where and how feasible interventions can take place. A framework for change provides us with the basis for developing a map of feasibility. To define a framework for change, we combine restrictions and opportunities for urban development.

Some natural features might represent restrictions for spatial change; however, squatter developments usually occupy areas unsuitable for urban development. In any urban area, environmental restrictions that would force displacement should be kept untouched. Communities are resistant to relocation, and only after environmental problems severely affect them do they accept moving.

Both the built environment and the open space include restrictions and opportunities for spatial change. Accessibility can affect opportunities for change. Because supplying building materials to interior areas is an enormous task in dense squatter developments, change may be too laborious. Proximity to roads allows a supply of building materials, but if roads are far away, the only means for transporting building materials is to carry them uphill via stairs.

Growth and substitution

In high-density squatter developments, change can occur through urban growth or substitution. High-density areas provide few possibilities for horizontal expansion; therefore, urban growth occurs mainly through a vertical increase of the built.

Substituting pieces, such as removing and renewing existing dwellings, is part of the planned process for growth and improvement. Because vertical growth depends on building height, and substitution of urban pieces depends on typologies, possibilities for changing the urban form depend on individual building heights and built group typologies. For example, depending on their height, existing buildings can change by increasing their number of floors. Substitution of detached dwellings is easy; however, typologies such as blocks of clustered dwellings are strong barriers for substitution.

The scarcity of urban space forces improvement plans to focus on substituting pieces and reviewing the open space of public passages to identify every small possibility for locating new activities. The only ways to build new roads or extend existing ones are through substituting existing buildings and determining typologies for open space that are more or less feasible for changing.

URBAN INTERVENTIONS

The goal of a proposal for urban interventions is to present a new scenario for the urban built environment. We initially propose improvements for the urban fabric and the open space system separately; however, a general improvement plan requires integrating both proposals.

We use the feasibility map to define where and how to improve the urban fabric and the open space. The feasibility map shows possible areas for changing the urban fabric and identifies areas for extending the pedestrian system or the road network. Areas unsuitable for development, but densely occupied, are targets for future relocation and are considered long-term urban interventions.

Site evaluation and poverty conditions of the built define the type and dimension of urban interventions. To achieve the community's desired levels of quality of life, proposed urban interventions must fit the conditions of the site while overcoming the more critical poverty conditions.

Urban design criteria

In general, urban design proposals pursue integrating the informal settlement with the planned city by balancing the quality of life conditions in the barrio with the surrounding areas. When the guiding principles of improvement are rooted in urban form and community capacities, the physical and social values of the community will be preserved. Referential elements, natural features, vernacular building codes, and social subdivisions are some of the values that need protection.

Preserving physical and social values means making minimum interventions. We do not consider expropriation a just policy for obtaining land. We propose expropriation only for environmental protection purposes when clear aggressions to the environment have occurred. Making minimum interventions requires that we pinpoint urban improvement and build within the built, especially whenever land is scarce. Recommended combinations for spatial change in high-density settlements are vertical growth and insertions of buildings whenever vacant land is available. In addition, building within the built is an urban intervention that preserves urban residents' memories.

CASE STUDIES

Every squatter development has its own character. Even though upgrading plans can share goals and design elements, they can have very different approaches and physical responses. To illustrate this, we return to the two barrios we discussed in chapter 4: Petare and Los Claveles.

The available data determines what type of site analyses can be done and what the proposals can include. In Petare we based our analysis on groups of buildings as a spatial unit. In Los Claveles we analyzed each dwelling separately. Proposals for Petare relied on replacing existing buildings. For Los Claveles we proposed inserting fragments of new development on vacant land at advantageous locations.

Proposal for Petare

Petare has a very dense urban occupation with little or no land for locating new facilities. The settlement has severe infrastructure problems. The network of water pipelines and sewers in the upper areas has been built with low-quality material by many different dwellers, which has produced widespread leaking that affects the terrain stability. Pipeline tracing is not mapped and the pedestrian stairs also function as drainage channels. In general, accessibility is very difficult; however, the central interior areas are the most severely affected.

The primary improvements that the community requested were related to accessibility, urban facilities, and infrastructure. The community was also unsatisfied with drainage and solid waste disposal.

The analysis we carried out, following the steps described in previous chapters, gave us a clear picture of the physical and social possibilities for change. This information became the foundation for developing proposals for the Petare urban fabric and open space system.

Developing proposals

The first step in the proposal process is developing a feasibility map. To identify what is feasible for urban interventions, we reviewed the possibilities for changing the built form. In addition to the built, we reviewed the existing system of open spaces and their possibilities for change. Removing and improving existing dwellings changes the built form and also affects the geometry of the open space. We used the feasibility map to propose extending existing access roads and laying new roads that could reach inaccessible areas.

Changing the built environment

To determine whether it was possible to replace buildings, we studied typologies of the built. Possibilities for changing built groups were graded from hard to soft, with two intermediate categories. Hard defines areas that are difficult to change without disrupting the built environment. Soft describes easy-to-change areas that preserve the existing order.

We identified hard and soft areas using the typologies map. For each typology, we associated a minor or major possibility for change, obtaining the following categories:

- ❖ Category 1 or soft areas: mixture of detached and twin houses
- ❖ Category 2 or medium soft areas: predominantly row houses
- ❖ Category 3 or medium hard areas: predominantly branched blocks
- ❖ Category 4 or hard areas: compact blocks

Figure 5-1 shows a map of hard and soft areas. Categories of hard and very hard areas define a preliminary threshold for spatial change.

To determine height change of the built, we used the map of existing building heights and graded changing possibilities from hard to soft, with one intermediate category. Hard areas are difficult to change for two reasons: (1) either buildings have reached their maximum

FIGURE 5-1
Hard and soft areas.

Map by Rosario C. Giusti de Pérez and assistants.

height of four floors, or (2) they are located in areas difficult to access. Areas that combine average heights of one floor and good accessibility are graded as soft.

Change and accessibility

Whether an area can change depends on whether it can be accessed. Areas easier to access are more likely to improve in the short run. Very difficult access can freeze improvement.

We measured distance to roads to establish grades of accessibility. Adjacency to roads provides good accessibility. We created a feasibility map (figure 5-2) by combining categories of hard and soft (figure 5-1) with adjacency to existing roads—this gave us major or minor possibilities for change.

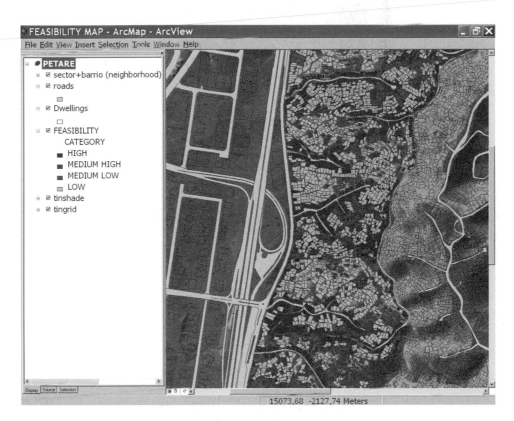

FIGURE 5-2
Feasibility map.

Map by Rosario C. Giusti de Pérez and assistants.

Change and typology of open space

We identified types of public open space and their possibilities for locating new activities. Combining information about geometry, position, and the function of open space, we established the following types:

❖ Road intersections
❖ Widened pedestrian spaces adjacent to access roads
❖ Disorganized areas with small vacant spaces, adjacent to roads

Each type of open space holds different possibilities to be molded or expanded. Typology does not define minor or major possibilities for change; it simply points out what kind of change is adequate. Whether open space can be changed depends on its location and geometric characteristics.

Residual space that appears as irregular geometry can be widened and improved. Weaving spaces also produces more leftover space. In some cases, intersections of open space provide possibilities for adding road returns. Road intersections appear as potential activity centers. Points at the dead ends of penetration roads appear as potential returns. Possible interior connectors exist where pedestrian space widens adjacent to access roads. Figure 5-3 shows different types of spaces that could be expanded to accommodate new urban uses.

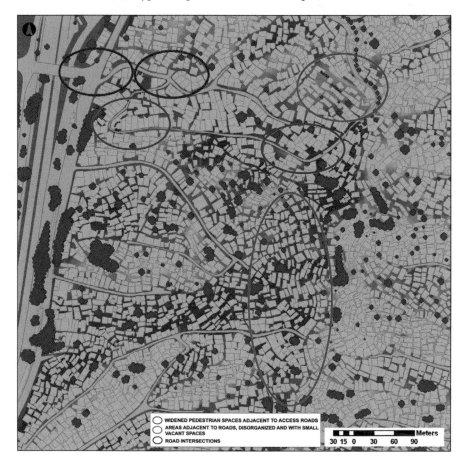

FIGURE 5-3

Spaces that could accommodate new urban uses.

Design by Rosario C. Giusti de Pérez.

The urban design proposal

We used GIS to develop the feasibility map (figure 5-2), which guided all plans for interventions described previously, plus the design of development regulations. Our urban design proposal includes a combined approach for horizontal extensions of very small dimensions, vertical growth of existing educational and health facilities, and substitution of selected pieces. We used the feasibility map as the basis for identifying where to include horizontal extensions.

To provide access to the interior areas of the settlement, we proposed two network scenarios: a continuous north–south axis to connect interior areas or a succession of interior penetrations initiated in the north and south peripheral roads. Illustrating both scenarios, the feasibility map (figure 5-2) showed that the north–south settlement crossing had a big impact on areas classified as nonfeasible for interventions (figure 5-4). Providing a continuous road to connect all barrios would require removing more than five hundred dwellings.

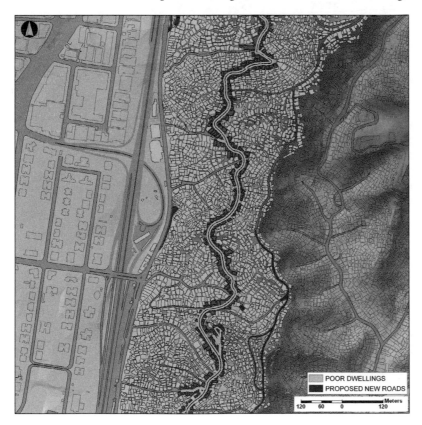

FIGURE 5-4
Proposed north–south route in Petare.

Map by Ramón A. Pérez.

Successions of inroad penetrations minimized the length of the trail, which reduced direct impacts on the built areas; however, this road system was not continuous and required a series of switchbacks. The urban design team chose to reinforce the existing branch-type road system. We proposed a succession of inroad penetrations that would have a minimal impact.

Whenever possible, we made good use of multiple dead-end roads, extending and including end returns or cul-de-sacs (figure 5-5). We organized the space around a cul-de-sac to incorporate small community services such as health-care centers, and turned return areas into local activity centers.

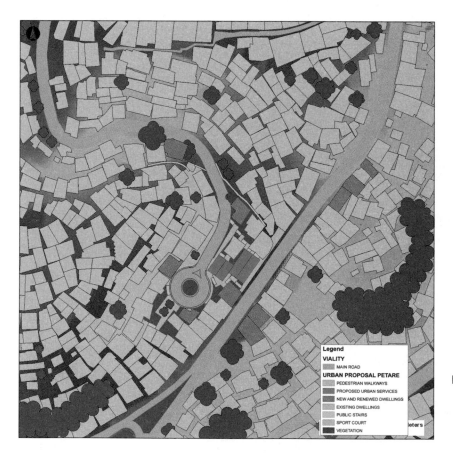

Legend

VIALITY
  MAIN ROAD

URBAN PROPOSAL PETARE
  PEDESTRIAN WALKWAYS
  PROPOSED URBAN SERVICES
  NEW AND RENEWED DWELLINGS
  EXISTING DWELLINGS
  PUBLIC STAIRS
  SPORT COURT
  VEGETATION

FIGURE 5-5
Solutions for
dead-end roads.

*Design by Rosario C.
Giusti de Pérez.*

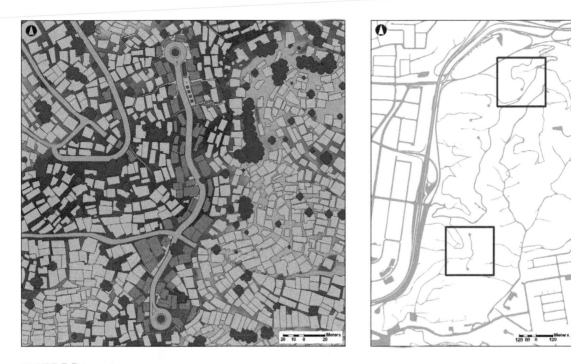

FIGURE 5-5 *(cont.)*
Solutions for dead-end roads.

Design by Rosario C. Giusti de Pérez.

We organized residual space generated by improvement interventions and integrated it into the existing open space to develop plazas or widen roads and pathways. We used residual space larger than 50 square meters for new housing or community services. Another solution for adding community facilities was to reuse them and vertically grow the existing buildings.

All urban interventions proposed by the plan respected the spirit of the place, understood as a social system of relations and a scale of small and well-defined open spaces (figure 5-6). Working together, technicians and a group of community members defined guidelines that were later submitted to the entire community for approval in an open assembly. Community members expressed what was important to them and what they wanted to preserve. Their desires were supported in the urban proposal. For example, buildings that the community wanted to preserve were renovated by adding floors and refurbishing facades (figure 5-7).

The pedestrian system of stairs and sidewalks was improved and extended to include new elevated sidewalks that would allow pedestrians to access the neighborhood and circulate next to the adjacent highway (Petare-Guarenas, shown in figure 5-4 running north–south and defining the west limit of the settlement). Continuities within the pedestrian system were reinforced and linked to the cul-de-sac system.

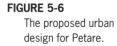

FIGURE 5-6

The proposed urban design for Petare.

Design by Rosario C. Giusti de Pérez.

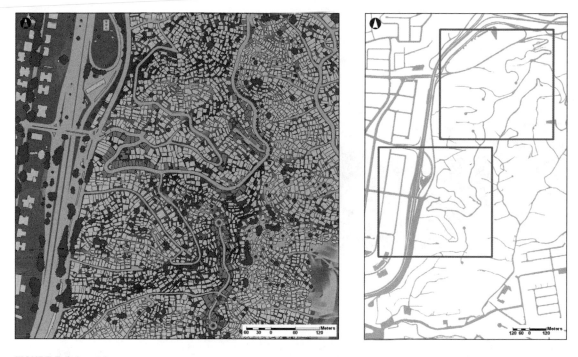

FIGURE 5-6 *(cont.)*
The proposed urban design for Petare.

Design by Rosario C. Giusti de Pérez.

All urban interventions proposed by the plan respected the spirit of the place, understood as a social system of relations and a scale of small and well-defined open spaces (figure 5-6). Working together, technicians and a group of community members defined guidelines that were later submitted to the entire community for approval in an open assembly. Community members expressed what was important to them and what they wanted to preserve. Their desires were supported in the urban proposal. For example, buildings that the community wanted to preserve were renovated by adding floors and refurbishing facades (figure 5-7).

FIGURE 5-7

Existing school building in Petare, before and after vertical growth proposal.

Photo and design by Rosario C. Giusti de Pérez and assistants.

PROPOSAL FOR LOS CLAVELES

The settlement of Los Claveles is located on a hillside that is densely occupied in the lower area, but less so as it moves up (figure 5-8). In 1999 during a landslide, part of the settlement and the access road to the upper areas was washed away. Water courses surround and run across the settlement dividing occupation in the upper areas.

FIGURE 5-8

General characteristics of the urban occupation in Los Claveles.

Three-dimensional map by Rosario C. Giusti de Pérez and Ramón A. Pérez; basemap image of Maiqutía and a proposed land development for Barrios Los Claveles courtesy of Instituto Geográfico Simón Bolívar, Cartografía Estado Vargas.

Los Claveles lacks all community facilities. The surrounding city provides recreational, educational, and health services for the residents. Sewers are nonexistent and water supply is irregular.

Our main goals for improving Los Claveles were related to access, solid waste disposal, recovery of deteriorated urban scenes, and adequate infrastructure for water drainage. The lack of roads to the upper areas makes an oppressive daily effort for many, especially the elderly and disabled. Residents expressed their desire to recover some areas that were partially destroyed in the landslide. They wanted planners to improve existing built areas, renew facades, and clean public space.

Developing proposals

In Los Claveles, possibilities and restrictions for change depend primarily on terrain characteristics. Topography is the strongest barrier to development. More than 70 percent of the settlement is located on slopes where grades exceed 30 percent.

Categories from the restrictions and opportunity map were translated to interventions that were more or less feasible. The feasibility map helped us determine locations for new community centers and the layout of new access roads to the upper areas.

Poverty maps were a basic reference for timing interventions and defining spatial change. Addressing the built resource, public space, and the urban scene, complemented with environmental fitness, allowed us to measure and map the spatial poverty.

Approaching change

Making changes in Los Claveles means organizing the existing occupation and proposing infill development wherever the topography allows it. Infill development includes roads, community facilities, and housing. Recovering abandoned buildings and residual space for community use was also part of the improvement proposals.

Community meetings in different barrio neighborhoods verified that residents wanted a better quality environment. Improving facades to achieve a better urban scene, considered by some as useless makeup, is actually important for communities. They want to be full citizens, and becoming full citizens means living a daily life in an urban habitat that has the attractive appearance of a finished environment, rather than the usual unfinished aspect predominant in this type of settlement.

Restrictions for increased accessibility depend on the possibilities for extending the road network from the surrounding areas. To increase accessibility, we identified possible extensions of the road layout, based on the map of hard and soft areas (figure 5-1). Road extensions through soft areas are more feasible than extensions that have to cross hard areas; therefore, to minimize impact, extensions were restricted to paths through soft areas.

The urban design proposal

We based our proposal to improve Los Claveles on a new road system that would provide access to existing residential areas and to new urban services located in the upper areas. The plan proposes retracing and extending the south access road to encircle the settlement. In the upper east area, the road becomes a peripheral limit with some east–west interior penetration. Accessible areas adjacent to roads were good locations for the community centers demanded by residents. Figure 5-9 shows proposed urban interventions, highlighting a proposed community center for the upper areas.

FIGURE 5-9

Proposed urban interventions with a detailed view of a proposed community center for the upper areas.

Three-dimensional map by Rosario C. Giusti de Pérez and Ramón A. Pérez.

We submitted a proposal for a cable car that would provide passenger and merchandise transportation to the community. This cable car was designed to transport waste disposal during special hours. To trace an efficient route, we concentrated our analysis on the central area. Available open space and minor steep slopes helped us decide the route (figure 5-10).

We reinforced the urban design plan with proposals to recover deteriorated urban scenes, such as the proposal shown in figure 5-11.

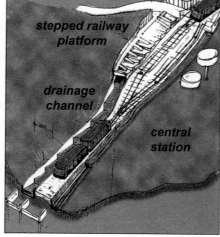

FIGURE 5-10

Proposed route for cable car.

Three-dimensional map by Rosario C. Giusti de Pérez and Ramón A. Pérez. Proposals by architect José Esposito.

FIGURE 5-11
A proposed community meeting place built over an abandoned slab.

Photos by Rosario C. Giusti de Pérez. Proposal design by Francisco Pérez Giusti.

GUIDELINES FOR URBAN PROPOSALS

We recommend the following guidelines when developing urban design proposals for squatter developments:

- ❖ Urban design proposals must integrate the settlement with the larger city by balancing quality of life conditions with the surrounding environment.
- ❖ Integration between squatter developments and their adjacent cities must preserve the existing spatial and social systems of relations within the settlement. Any urban intervention needs to promote social and physical cohesion.
- ❖ The urban design proposal must benefit the physical, social, and economic conditions of the site.
- ❖ Proposals should maintain key features of the urban scene, since the features provide a singularity of appearance, which is highly meaningful to the communities.
- ❖ Improvement interventions should provide a balanced fit between the built environment and proposed actions, avoiding scale aggressions or monumental solutions.
- ❖ The proposed urban scene must integrate new elements with the collective memories of the residents.

In the next chapter, we describe how to manage the development and implementation of an improvement project with GIS.

6

MANAGING IMPROVEMENT
PROJECTS WITH GIS

The complexity of social and physical relations in squatter developments requires that we manage efficiently the entire process of improvement plan development and execution. This means using tools to keep track of the multiple tasks involved and the many people responsible for carrying them out.

Planners often use project management software, usually Microsoft Office Project or other software that creates critical path method (CPM) or Gantt charts. The purpose of such software, of course, is to produce diagrams that show milestones of building progress, demonstrating whether planners have a handle on the building progress. In the building industry, project management software usually is used to keep track of all the detailed jobs involved in one single construction process, such as building a school or a hospital. In these cases, geography is not very important. But to keep track of many building efforts at several sites, or even in several cities, using normal project management software is not the best way to geographically visualize where and when progress is being made.

In developing countries, planning agencies in charge of improvement plans seldom use project management software to monitor and report activities during plan execution. Yet software that can use building completion data to track progress and geographically identify significant issues and problems will minimize project risks. A software program that can totally manage an improvement plan leads to more efficient, more effective, and more successful outcomes.

To keep track of all tasks and their building phases, we can use software like Microsoft's project management desktop products; however, that software performs without a spatial context. To track ongoing improvements, not only as phases and tasks, but as a system that can locate and map progress, we developed a GIS interface to work with Microsoft Office Project. This provides a clear picture of when and where improvement plans for a squatter development are being accomplished.

MANAGING IMPROVEMENT IN SQUATTER DEVELOPMENTS

Improvement interventions in squatter developments involve a myriad of small and medium construction tasks such as building new stairs, paving walkways, building sewerage pipe collectors, deviating and casting surface drainage, building sports playgrounds, schools, health facilities, and so on. A joint effort between planners and the community can lead to identifying hundreds of these small, required improvements and even larger projects.

Some improvements, especially the small ones, can be built by the community itself. Larger improvement projects can be contracted to small engineering enterprises.

Occasionally a major building or infrastructure, such as a new road, school, or health center, requires the participation of a major construction firm. In Venezuela, planning agencies usually coordinate all the efforts and investments required to improve barrios. Many other agencies and public offices are identified as providers of solutions or financial help; however, most of the minor tasks are contracted to individuals or small building groups within the barrios.

GIS PROJECT MANAGEMENT FOR GOVERNANCE

Public projects need to adhere to governance at both the national and local levels. By definition, governance in the public sector is the ability to satisfy many public interests; therefore, governance includes the following:

- ❖ Community interests
- ❖ Committees
- ❖ Oversight
- ❖ Program and project review
- ❖ Decision-making bodies
- ❖ Voting
- ❖ Financial transparency
- ❖ Financial review

GIS can help make public projects visible, especially in the eyes of community and official institutions that finance improvements. Satisfying the rules of governance often means letting interested parties know how the improvement plan is progressing. Committee members and executives want to be able to look at a report quickly and tell whether or not a project is on target or in jeopardy—financially, or in terms of its schedule or scope.

The crucial thing is to make sure that reported information is as accurate as possible. Project reports presented to the community can display general progress of improvements; however, reports presented to institutions must provide more detailed information about progress and expenditures. Executives and corporate governors will quickly balk at incomplete or inaccurate reports. Questions need be answered about when and where, how much has been spent, who is responsible, and, above all, whether the community is satisfied.

Another aspect scrutinized under the governance microscope is financial reporting, and accuracy is paramount here. Managers on public projects will likely be asked to ensure that financial reporting conforms to the governing body's planned budget.

One of the most common reporting methods used to satisfy institutional governance members is the RAG scale (red, amber, and green), often referred to as the "stoplight metric." With just a glance someone can tell, at least theoretically, whether a project is on target (green), needs management attention (yellow), or is way off schedule (red).

GIS can make use of the stoplight metric to render reports, making it easy to see if the task is yellow heading for a stop, or cruising through the green lights. Again, in order for this information to be useful, the information behind the metric needs to be accurate. Using GIS can show where management attention is required.

The project management process

We use GIS to monitor and review the progress of building improvements. To do this, the planning team needs to collect data to assess the current state of the project. The activities of the planning team usually include the following:

- ❖ Geographically locating the improvements or completed tasks
- ❖ Reviewing the completed activities
- ❖ Identifying milestones reached
- ❖ Identifying problems or issues
- ❖ Updating project schedules and progress information
- ❖ Updating budgets and variances

Project management software should be capable of the following tasks:

- ❖ Address issues
- ❖ Review change requests and make recommendations
- ❖ Prepare action plans
- ❖ Reschedule when necessary
- ❖ Allocate resources
- ❖ Add equipment and other resources

Figure 6-1 illustrates the project management process.

To manage complicated, multiscale improvement interventions, we design unique processes that fit the special needs of each project. Key elements of these processes include the following:

- ❖ A database that serves as a central repository for information about all changes and issues of concern, for example, a geodatabase
- ❖ A summary of information on the processes on a change request form or issue form;
- ❖ Configuration management processes

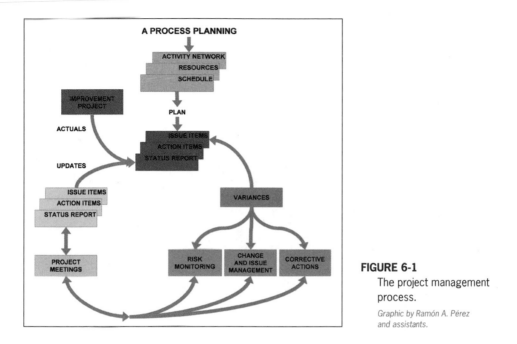

FIGURE 6-1

The project management process.

Graphic by Ramón A. Pérez and assistants.

❖ Assignment of a change manager, either the project manager or a member of the status tracking/review team
❖ Updated summary reports for the standard project status meetings
❖ Consistent and ongoing evaluation of changes, issues, and development of appropriate resolution and implementation strategies

A SYSTEM TO TRACK IMPROVEMENTS

We created a special system to track improvements and combined it with the ability to use time as a variable, a function available in the ArcGIS Tracking Analyst extension. The automated system handles the jobs of a project manager, with GIS centrally managing the tasks, costs, timing, and location of all improvements.

This tool requires a geographic location and a description of essential tasks for all the projects. For each task we identify subtasks, time frames, and individuals or entities responsible for their executions. Usually this requires the creation of several related tables. When the tables point to an improvement at a particular location, the program returns all subtasks needed to complete that improvement.

Applying this approach, we developed a system integrated with GIS for the barrio Palo Negro located in the city of Maracaibo, approximately five hundred miles west of Caracas. In the rest of this chapter we describe the system we developed for this project and show how planning agencies can use GIS to keep track of improvement efforts in different barrios.

Scales of improvement

Since 1992, governmental planning agencies in Venezuela have been working to integrate squatter developments into city structures. They usually describe urban scale improvements through sector plans and plans for physical units. A sector plan includes all areas of a city occupied by squatter developments. Physical planning units (PPU) cover groups of contiguous squatter developments located within the city. Both plans include improvements for several squatter developments.

A plan for an urban design unit (UDU) addresses improvement of smaller areas in one or two squatter developments, or part of a large one. A PPU contains plans for several UDUs. We also develop plans for condominium structures that describe areas occupied by small, organized community groups.

Even though a sector plan and a plan for physical units are both urban scale plans, the PPU embraces larger areas of a city. We apply two differing scale nominations to these plans—the general urban scale plan for sector plans and the intermediate urban scale for PPUs. Plans for urban design units are local scale plans, and condominium structure plans are community plans.

An investment improvement plan (IIP) summarizes the costs of all the improvement tasks for the city as a whole. Investments at all scales and the agencies responsible for each one of them are part of this plan.

GIS FOR MANAGING IMPROVEMENTS IN BARRIO PALO NEGRO

Throughout the administrative and managing phases involved in building improvements, we need to keep track of how much, where, and when progress is taking place. To do this, we can model time as a variable in the geodatabase, then collect completion dates at all scales of intervention. We also obtain information about task phasing and cyclic supervision of work completed at all levels.

With the planned building phases and dates for completed tasks, we use ArcGIS Tracking Analyst to dynamically show improvements taking place. Figure 6-2 provides a graphic view of investment improvement plans for each scale (general urban, intermediate

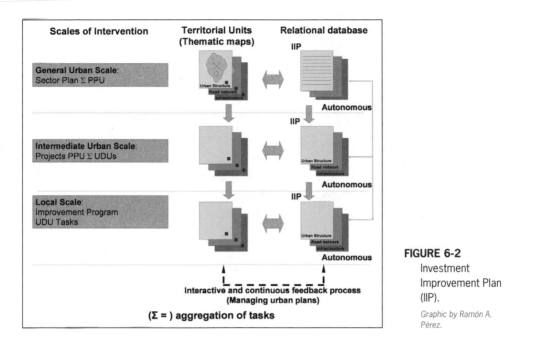

FIGURE 6-2

Investment
Improvement Plan
(IIP).

*Graphic by Ramón A.
Pérez.*

urban, and local) to simplify and explain the process. A box displays thematic maps showing urban structure, road networks, and urban services for each scale. The IIP (Investment Improvement Plan) box displays cost figures per task.

With scales of improvements defined and territorially located, we use GIS to summarize all the improvement tasks for the city as a whole. We can locate and assign required investments to political districts, local government agencies, and social services acting within the city. Figure 6-3 shows the city as a subdivision of political units or districts (parishes, in the case of Maracaibo) and how the plan works with the help of GIS. At this level we summarize the investments required by each district, how many people are being served, how many square meters are being built, and so on. The map on the left shows the municipal subdivision (Municipio Maracaibo and Municipio San Francisco) and the map on the right shows parish subdivisions for the whole urban area. Within a parish we locate the physical units and display data for different coverages.

At the intermediate level, GIS can handle and summarize information to show investments for physical planning units (PPU) and urban design units (UDU). This results from visualizing improvement tasks as tables that describe job phasing, timing, and costs. We can also create information fields for the contract, responsible individuals or entities, and the completed tasks.

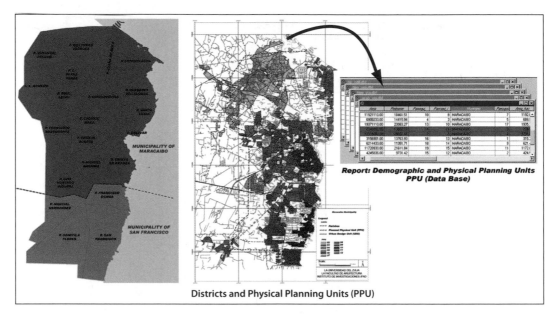

Districts and Physical Planning Units (PPU)

FIGURE 6-3

Subdivisions at differing scales for the city of Maracaibo.

Map by Ramón A. Pérez and assistants.

For Palo Negro, we developed tables associated with the physical unit and the urban design unit. From these tables, we created a plan for urban interventions (Plan de Actuaciones Urbanísticas) that summarized all interventions required by both the PPU and UDU. To date, part of this plan has been successfully implemented, though some improvements are awaiting financing approval.

A well-designed database can efficiently manage all levels of intervention and improvement and establish the relationships required to create the summary reports, either as listings or as maps. This allows us to display the progress being made in the improvement process. Using 3D images can improve communication with the community.

The map and charts in figure 6-4 summarize a GIS system acting at the medium scale. On the map, the blue highlighted area identifies the limits of the UDU Palo Negro. The chart at the top gives statistics for the entire physical planning unit with the study area data highlighted in yellow. The lower chart displays the investments required for developing programs such as roads, services, and others in the short, medium, and long terms.

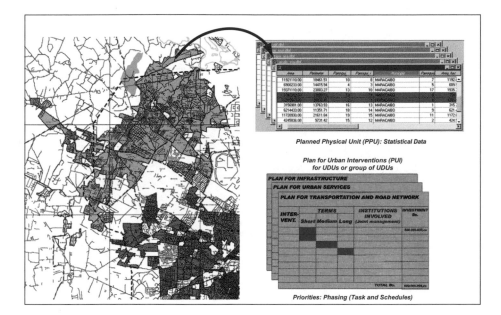

Planned Physical Unit (PPU): Statistical Data

Plan for Urban Interventions (PUI)
for UDUs or group of UDUs

FIGURE 6-4

GIS systems acting at the intermediate scale.

Maps by Ramón A. Pérez and assistants.

At the local level, we use GIS to report a detailed program of interventions, showing who is responsible for each task, the level of investment, the priorities for development, and the phases of all the improvements. If properly conceived and planned, GIS can help public agencies, local government, and organized communities manage and follow up on the improvement plan. GIS can facilitate communication toward the main goal of the whole process: improving the community's quality of life. Figure 6-5 shows that, at the local level, GIS can report improvements geographically and chart the phasing and schedules for all tasks, jobs, and improvement interventions.

Figure 6-5 shows where various urban design projects in Palo Negro are located. The adjacent chart displays information about programs to supply and improve urban services, roads, and infrastructure. For each program, the chart displays activity type and location, institutions responsible for developing the project and execution costs. Costs for each phase are displayed and classified as immediate, or short- or medium-term.

With ArcGIS, users can create cycling models and develop what-if scenarios at all scales. Using ArcGIS Spatial Analyst with ModelBuilder allows planners to examine alternative

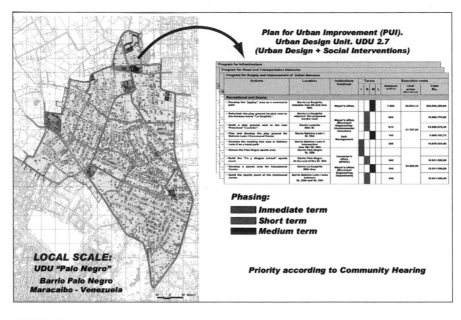

FIGURE 6-5

GIS at the local scale.

Maps by Rosario C. Giusti de Pérez and assistants.

scenarios. Because of connections established in the geodatabase, ArcGIS serves as a powerful project management tool. It can manage the efforts of national large-scale public works for multiple projects at different scales and scopes. Figure 6-6 includes a map of the projects for the central urban axis and a chart specifying investment schedules for each project.

The following guidelines can help planners and others to successfully use GIS as a central project management tool:

❖ Urban scale information can be handled by the city or local government; however, information at the local level is owned and controlled by the community.

❖ GIS can help communities visualize ongoing improvements. This helps stimulate communities to take direct action toward solving their problems.

❖ Maps should be produced at different stages throughout the improvement plan.

❖ The database should be updated or modified by those who manage the improvement plan.

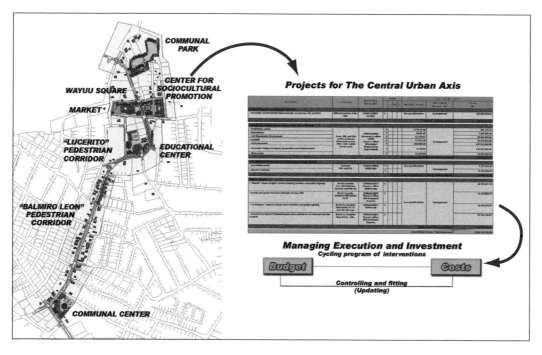

FIGURE 6-6
Levels of interventions.
Maps by Rosario C. Giusti de Pérez and assistants.

❖ Analysis, follow-up, and management of urban interventions generate new information at all levels. As soon as improvements are accepted by the community, information must be added to the geodatabase.

❖ Continuous participation of the communities is required during analysis, follow-up, and management of improvement projects.

In the next chapter, we describe how we involve barrio residents in the processes of development and implementation of improvement projects.

7

COMMUNITY PARTICIPATION:
A REQUIREMENT FOR
SUSTAINABILITY

In this chapter we describe our experience working side-by-side with poor communities to improve their neighborhoods. For us, this process began simply when we asked residents for information. It ended with the community participating in managing the improvement proposals. To guarantee sustainable solutions, the values and agendas of the squatter development's residents must be incorporated into the planning and policy-making process.

COMMUNITY PARTICIPATION

At the start of the planning process, planning agencies and municipal councils usually identify and contact community leaders. Representatives of the planning agencies officially present the planning team to the community. After that, we, as consultants, are on our own, organizing communities to involve them in the improvement process. Our goal is to make sure that everyone living within that space will benefit from improvements.

With community leaders we schedule a series of general meetings to which we invite the entire community. Meetings take place in schools, pedestrian paths or streets that are wide enough to accommodate the group, or sometimes in residents' homes. At these meetings, we interview residents to understand the real boundaries of the community.

At the first meeting, we explore issues and ideas residents have about improving their community. We promote discussions with the goal of reaching agreements about priorities. As meetings continue, communities usually build a sense of ownership with the project and begin to participate more fully. By the end, participation leads to a joint decision-making process and, therefore, to a successful project. Figure 7-1 shows meetings with indigenous communities of Palo Negro, the Maracaibo squatter development whose planning process we discussed in chapter 6.

We have found that it is impossible to define social information that is spatially related without community participation. Residents' knowledge of their daily problems helps planners, and we feel it's vital that professionals realize that they alone cannot provide all the answers.

Likewise, communities need a full understanding of improvement proposals. It is not enough for a technical team to propose, solve, and apply solutions to a problem. For communities to support and be committed to development plans, they need to understand proposed solutions. Once residents understand proposals, their participation can help professionals modify the project agenda in terms of topics and timing.

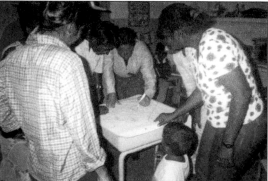

FIGURE 7-1

Meetings with indigenous communities of Palo Negro, Maracaibo.

Photos by Rosario C. Giusti de Pérez and assistants.

CREATING COMMUNITY ASSOCIATIONS

In Venezuela, neighborhood associations have recognized legal rights; therefore, creating community associations is the initial step whenever planning for urban development projects. Venezuelan agencies promote the creation of community associations that combine concepts of social domain and physical space. These groups, called *estructuras condominiales* (which translates as condominium structures), allow communities to benefit from common services (water supply, electricity, and access roads) and become responsible for shared facilities and urban space. In local squatter development groups, we saw an opportunity to apply this type of association where space is given a social value beyond the usual physical one.

In condominium organizations, communities control and maintain their environment. Community participation is important not only for reaching a regular and sufficient service level but also for negotiating reasonable rates for services. Usually squatter developments pay a fixed rate for water supply, negotiated between the community and the agency providing the service. Organized communities take on responsibilities for maintaining adequate levels of water consumption, avoiding water waste, and maintaining the rates negotiated with the service provider.

Even though residents in traditional condominiums and squatter development condominiums both share space and facilities, fundamental differences between them exist. In traditional condominiums, social relations between residents may not exist. In squatter developments, those are usually required conditions for establishing condominium status. In squatter developments, a potential condominium is a shared residential area with strong identity elements where residents are attached to the place and have an informal neighborhood association. These characteristics provide a basis for beginning to organize community groups.

Changes in perspective

To go deeply into the daily needs of poor communities, we find it best to approach small groups of residents. Subtle differences in daily needs can be perceived between small groups, so to manage, supply, and maintain basic urban services, we have to identify the smallest social cell linked to a place.

A **social cell** is a group of residents that share a territory, social relations, and common open space. Because we define a social cell as a social domain concept, we use it to identify the network of relations, individual responsibilities, and family coresponsibilities. Naturally, families are central elements in community life.

Defining the social cell allows us to identify a space of collective responsibility and preserve the invisible psychological links that residents have to places and neighbors. An association such as a condominium strengthens communities to move toward legalizing land tenure, negotiate with government institutions that provide urban services, develop a participative plan for managing the needs and demands of their community, and build internal regulations to control use, management, and behavior within the semiprivate or public spaces.

Criteria for establishing condominium boundaries

Communal spaces are where residents share the activities of daily life. These include access routes, urban facilities, and infrastructure. Environmental and physical events such as water courses or pedestrian paths comprise communal spaces, which are required for defining community boundaries. We must be sure to include within the community area, however, social and cultural aspects linked to community identity. Small spaces where neighbors meet, a big tree that provides shade, a religious monument that distinguishes an area, and signs indicating names for streets and pedestrian stairs are all elements linked to community life.

The definition of communal space cannot be imposed, but it can be established with residents' participation. Residents' perceptions of their space are more important than the physical characteristics of that space. In squatter developments, strong emotional relationships exist between spaces and people. Shared space is the best way to promote social ties and side-by-side living.

To establish physical limits, planners need to consider combinations of natural, social, and built elements. Peripheral dwellings require special analysis. Drainage channels, stairs, paths, and other built elements can become borders. A shared hydrographic basin is a fundamental geographic element and water courses are separations that affect social relations.

COMMUNITY ORGANIZATION

In assemblies and workshops, residents review the boundaries of their communal space and confirm that all significant urban elements are included. Continuing these assemblies throughout project development allows planners to continue obtaining information from residents about community problems, the feasibility of proposed solutions, and public aspirations. It also permits planners to detect conflicts among and between neighbors and local community groups. These conflicts generally relate to property limits, space organization, and rights of use of public space. Solutions to conflicts can be approached through improvement changes that establish clear limits between private and public space and define uses and users.

Final proposals for organizing space result from negotiations between the planning team, who know the technical possibilities, and the community, who know the local social and environmental conditions. To guarantee the success of a condominium structure, projects must do the following:

❖ Assign priorities to the social character of the project, thereby strengthening community organization.

❖ Through community meetings and workshops, reach agreements for defining priorities of urban improvement, developing design guidelines, and establishing behavioral rules.

❖ Include residents in the early stages of the project and continue until it ends. This provides communities with a complete understanding of the improvement plan and creates commitment to their project.

❖ Create responsibility, reliability, and solidarity with community residents to promote internal agreements about maintenance of existing and proposed spaces.

❖ Subordinate physical interventions to the possibilities of community participation.

❖ Respect the existing cultural heritage and support valuable local building solutions, thereby minimizing formal dependencies from institutions.

We distribute information about boundaries and project goals on flyers and posters. After this general advertising process, communities are, once again, organized at meetings with the planning group. The main goal of these meetings is to create a neighborhood association that will be responsible for following the development of the urban interventions. Once communities are organized as an association, they become autonomous management cells with negotiation capability. Improvement projects can become a negotiation between the condominium structure and the planning agency. The strength and stability of a community institutional group provides the possibility of converting desires, through actions, into a changed urban scene.

CASE STUDY OF COMMUNITY PARTICIPATION

Planning agencies in Venezuela chose three small squatter development areas to promote community involvement and management of their improvement activities. Community structures were organized for the first time in 2004. The planning process included developing both an improvement project and guidelines for social behavior and we developed these in parallel, with continuous community participation. Approval of a final ruling document was achieved in meetings with community leaders.

At community meetings and workshops, residents were organized to do the following:

- ❖ Achieve agreements on priority needs
- ❖ Assign different groups to be responsible for tasks related to improvement projects
- ❖ Develop a strategy for achieving project goals
- ❖ Design development and behavioral rules for the condominium

Proposals for improvement included making a diagnosis of the physical and social environments. Two parallel steps were carried out at the initial stages of the diagnosis: organizing residents and defining accurate community boundaries. The planning agency provided preliminary boundaries, but final limits of the spatial units were defined using maps and photographs and information provided by residents. The second task was defining the parcel limits. Parcels with no ownership were included in a land-legalizing procedure.

We developed proposals for a series of improvement projects for urban space, pedestrian passages, water supply, sewers, and drainage. Maps to identify networks of drinking water supplies and sewers started out simply as sketches displaying the main pipes; the network showing water access to dwellings was nonexistent. We traced access lines and assessed the conditions of water supply, sewers, and drainage using information provided by each dweller.

Legal consultants designed guidelines for urban development and social behavior with continuous community participation. Legal consultants were also responsible for preparing property documents for those parcels without ownership. After several meetings with community leaders, a final ruling document was approved. We managed this planning process using GIS, which helped us keep track of multiple tasks related to regulating landownership, community participation, agreements, and building permissions.

DOÑA EVANGELISTA: LOCATION AND CHARACTERISTICS

The condominium structure of Doña Evangelista, in the barrio of Petare, provides one example of designing a community-supported plan. Doña Evangelista is located in Petare's Barrio 24 de Julio, facing the Petare-Guarenas highway and easily identified by a retaining wall that defines the area (figure 7-2). Doña Evangelista is a community of twenty buildings that lodge thirty-five families, with an average size of five persons per family. Nearly all the families were founders of the barrio years ago. Sharing history has created strong community ties and united them in making requests for improvement.

Existing external and internal elements provide a clear understanding of the spatial unit. For example, the retaining wall provides access from the highway to a small public space and from there to surrounding dwellings. Direct access to dwellings and public transportation provides a higher quality of life than in the interior communities. A relevant internal element is a school that is visible from outside the neighborhood. This building, integrated in a continuous public facade that serves as a background screen, reinforces the identity of the community (figure 7-3).

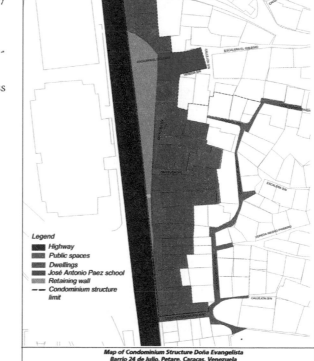

Legend
- Highway
- Public spaces
- Dwellings
- José Antonio Paez school
- Retaining wall
- Condominium structure limit

Map of Condominium Structure Doña Evangelista
Barrio 24 de Julio, Petare, Caracas, Venezuela

FIGURE 7-2

Map of Doña Evangelista.

Map by Rosario C. Giusti de Pérez and assistants.

FIGURE 7-3
West facade of Doña Evangelista.

Photo by Rosario C. Giusti de Pérez and assistants.

A condominium plan for Doña Evangelista

The plan for Doña Evangelista pursued improving quality of life in the area and organizing the residents into a condominium structure association. Community members led the process of site analysis and residents participated in the evaluation of the area. The following list resulted:

- ❖ The main social problem is unemployment.
- ❖ Land property problems are nonexistent. Residents are already involved in a process of legalizing landownership.
- ❖ The area lacks meeting and gathering spaces.
- ❖ Individuals lack the initiative to organize and maintain the existing public space.
- ❖ People expand their living space by increasing the number of floors in buildings. This anarchic vertical growth generates drainage and sewerage problems.
- ❖ People have a strong desire to create a neighbor association (*junta comunal*).
- ❖ Nearly all dwellings have water supply, electricity, and sewers. They have electric meters but no water meters. Water is priced on a fixed rate and every dwelling pays the same rate for water supply; however, unemployment in the community makes it difficult for some residents to pay that rate.

Opportunities and problems

Opportunities and problems specific to Doña Evangelista include the following:

❖ Direct access to public transportation makes the site attractive.

❖ The continuous group facade provides a clear definition of the urban space.

❖ A balcony-type, semipublic space promotes social interaction between residents.

❖ Dwelling consolidation provides lodging for several generations.

❖ The water supply system is precarious and periodical. The main pipeline is attached with wires to a balcony fence. The distribution network is erratic and pipelines are superficial and small. Since there are no water meters, consumption is high and residents don't bother fixing leaks. Water is supplied only two or three times a week.

❖ Sewer systems are underground and difficult to locate. Some downspouts from upper dwellings are superficial. According to residents, pipelines are thirty years old. That, combined with steep slopes, could produce a short-term collapse.

❖ Internal drainage is not a major problem; however, water from area drains flows toward the highway where it accumulates and creates a public health problem.

Condominium structure: subdivisions

Planning agencies assumed that residents in the clustered buildings would work together in a unique neighborhood association. A view from the highway gives an impression of wholeness based on the facade continuity; however, in meetings with community members, planners learned that residents had a strong sense of belonging to different social groups. Residents in the condominium area felt that they belonged to one of three different groups—one north and two south of an existing elementary school.

Planners agreed to establish a subcondominium for each group and develop, as an initial stage, a plan for the central subcondominium. Definition and legal organization of the three subcondominiums were achieved through community meetings (figure 7-4). Once each subcondominium was organized, the plan for the central subcondominium became the example to follow and behavior rules were welcomed by all residents of the condominiums.

Community-expressed desires

In interviews, community members stated that they wanted the improvements to accomplish the following:

❖ Provide channels to drain rain water.

❖ Organize and refurbish open space so they could use it as recreational areas, mainly for children.

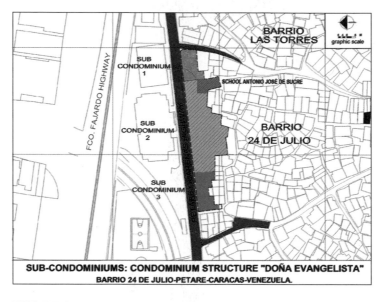

FIGURE 7-4

Subcondominiums in Doña Evangelista.

Map by Rosario C. Giusti de Pérez and assistants.

- ❖ Provide handrails for the main access stairway to improve circulation security.
- ❖ Provide public lighting because the lack of adequate light increases insecurity.
- ❖ Make aesthetic improvements. This was the major demand expressed by community members, especially young people. They felt this would change their poverty image and make a difference with the rest of the settlement.

Proposals for urban interventions

Proposals for improvement included interventions to infrastructure and the functioning and appearance of the subcondominium. Planners developed building specifications for each proposed public work.

Proposals for physical appearance and functioning included the following:

- ❖ Reinforcement and extension of the existing retaining wall, including landscape conditioning and a pedestrian connection with the existing school (figure 7-5).

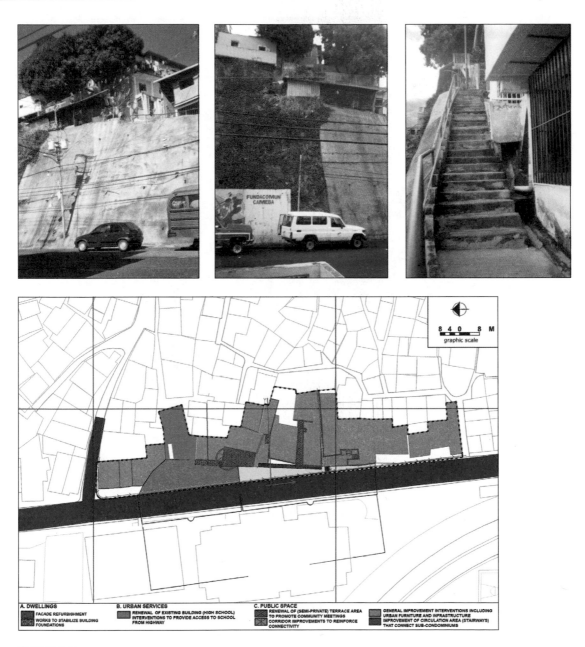

FIGURE 7-5

General required improvements.

Photos and map by Rosario C. Giusti de Pérez and assistants.

- ❖ Refurbishment of public space with new public lighting, substitution of public-space pavement, organization of surface levels, and relocation of access stairs to dwellings (figure 7-6).
- ❖ Facade improvements such as painting, roof gutters, and drain pipes (figure 7-7).
- ❖ Construction of a new access stairway to the subcondominium. This project includes a drainage channel parallel to the retaining wall and a special area for waste disposal (figures 7-8).

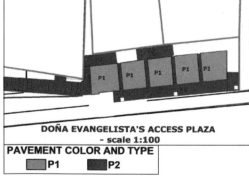

DOÑA EVANGELISTA'S ACCESS PLAZA
- scale 1:100
PAVEMENT COLOR AND TYPE
P1   P2

FIGURE 7-6

Public space improvements.

Photos, design, and map by Rosario C. Giusti de Pérez and assistants.

126

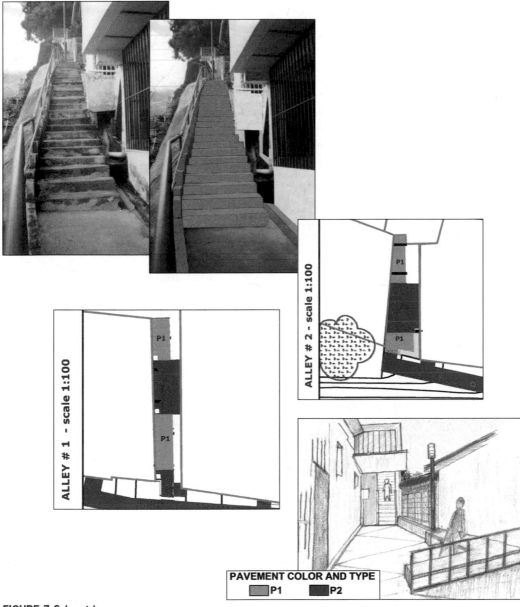

FIGURE 7-6 (cont.)
Public space improvements.

Photos, design, and map by Rosario C. Giusti de Pérez and assistants.

FIGURE 7-7
Proposals for facade improvement.

Photos and design by Rosario C. Giusti de Pérez and assistants.

7-7A Existing Urban Scene

7-7B Proposed Urban Scene

7-7C Existing Urban Scene

7-7D Proposed Urban Scene

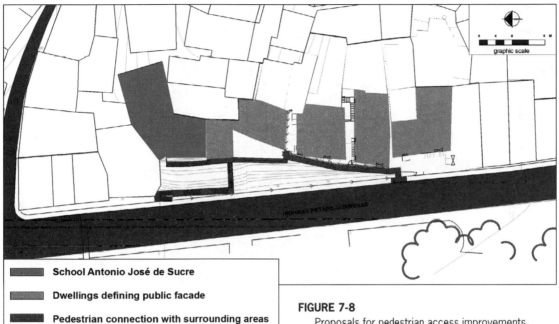

School Antonio José de Sucre

Dwellings defining public facade

Pedestrian connection with surrounding areas

FIGURE 7-8

Proposals for pedestrian access improvements.

Map by Rosario C. Giusti de Pérez and assistants.

We developed proposals for infrastructure projects to accomplish the following:

❖ Move the main water feeder underneath the main stairways and connect water supply to the city pipeline.

❖ Substitute the bundle-type superficial water supply system with an underground branched feeder.

❖ Promote agreements between the agency providing water and the community that would establish routes and fair service rates.

❖ Design the sewer collector beneath the main access stair. Provide a secondary branch water system to connect dwellings.

❖ Substitute the superficial pumping system with underground wastewater disposal lines;

❖ Design a drainage channel adjacent to the main access stair for rainwater discharge. Water accumulates during the rainy season, which makes access to the area difficult.

❖ Renew the drainage channel that runs along the highway.

Figures 7-9 and 7-10 illustrate the process of improvement.

FIGURE 7-9
A general view of the condominium facade refurbishment.

Photo by Rosario C. Giusti de Pérez.

FIGURE 7-10
Details of facade and stair improvements.

Photo by Rosario C. Giusti de Pérez.

Rules for the social and physical functioning of condominiums

To guarantee success, the planning team designed simple and easily understood rules for physical development and social behavior. To be successful, the residents needed to understand the guidelines and rules. The main source for rule design was site analysis and residents' information about their needs.

Social rules guide residents' behavior with other residents and with their living space. Communities usually accept guidelines for development and social behavior negotiated with local planning authorities. Communities themselves chose the word "behavior" for the set of social rules. Simple responsibility rules support maintenance of public facilities. A condominium-ruling document includes general and specific rules. General rules include definitions to make the document easily understandable. Terms such as lot, facade, attachment, slab, cantilevers, and so on, were described and explained at meetings with residents. Permitted and nonpermitted land use was fully described.

Behavior rules

The planning team and the neighborhood condominium association developed a document to guide residents' behavior. Rules included two types of controls, those related to living side-by-side with others and those related to the use, maintenance, and preservation of community spaces. To promote peace and solidarity between residents, the rules avoided sanctions.

Behavior rules included the following:

- ❖ All residents have access to condominium public areas. Urban furniture or crowds at the entrance to these areas are not allowed.
- ❖ Residents must protect their community from strangers who could endanger the security and functioning of the condominium area.
- ❖ Activities in private or public areas that produce noise have hours and intensity regulations.
- ❖ Consuming alcoholic beverages in public areas is not allowed.
- ❖ Waste can be disposed of only in specific places.
- ❖ Animal owners have special responsibilities.
- ❖ Daily cleaning is required for dwellings' front areas.
- ❖ Maintaining and cleaning public spaces is a shared responsibility.
- ❖ Festivities in common open space can only occur during special hours.

Physical rules

Physical rules guide building and renewal interventions and serve to protect public space. Some of these guidelines include the following:

- ❖ Enlargements adjacent to public space are not permitted.
- ❖ Cantilevers and balconies over public space are not permitted.
- ❖ Meters currently located on dwelling facades must be grouped and contained in specially built boxes.
- ❖ Building heights cannot exceed four floors. Vertical extensions are permitted in dwellings that have not reached the maximum height. No vertical extensions are permitted in existing buildings that already exceed height limits.
- ❖ To promote structural stability, floor and roof slabs must coincide whenever attached dwellings are renewed or enlarged.

GENERAL CONCLUSIONS

Planning for the poor succeeds when citizens participate and take direct action toward solving their problems. Residents need to be involved with a project so that both they and the planners understand it and its potential effects. Community participation can help right mismatches between technical proposals and community requirements. The capacity of an organized community to dialogue with the institutions that provide electricity and water allows residents to request the infrastructure improvements they want.

To ensure community participation and harmony between residents, groups should be small. Planning agencies usually identify a social unit based on spatial and social considerations. Sometimes planners need to make adjustments when communities identify more than one social unit or group within the spatial boundaries.

Displaying information graphically helps planners communicate plans and projects to residents; however, residents' full understanding and participation depends on a community-based contribution of knowledge. GIS promotes community contribution through an interactive process that allows residents to add relevant spatial information to the database and display its effect on improvement interventions. Involving community groups with GIS enhances their capacity to generate, manage, and communicate valuable spatial information hidden within the complexity of poor settlements.

BIBLIOGRAPHY

Arendt, Randall, Dodson Associates, and others. 1994. Rapid site assessment methodology. Conservation subdivision design process.

Borja, Jordi. April/May/June 2004. El Mercado dejado suelto es destructor de la ciudad. *Revista Tenia* número 4.

Castells, Manuel. 1996. *La era de la información 1. Economía, sociedad y cultura*. Madrid: Alianza Press.

Kozlowski, Jerzy, and J. T. Hudges. 1972. *Threshold analysis*. London: The Architectural Press.

McHarg, Ian L. 1969. *Design with nature*. Garden City, New York: American Museum of Natural History, Natural History Press.

Ministerio de Infraestructura. Consejo Nacional de la Vivienda (CONAVI). 1999. La habilitación física de zonas de barrios. Caracas, Venezuela.

Waisman, Marina. 1995. *La arquitectura descentrada*. Collection on Latin American History and Theory. Escala. Bogota Colombia. 119.

Zaremba, Piotr, and Jerzy Kozlowski. 1974. Lessons on urban planning: Threshold theory method. Szczecin, Poland: Szczecin University of Technology.

Related titles from ESRI Press

Mapping Global Cities: GIS Methods in Urban Analysis
ISBN 978-1-58948-143-5

GIS for the Urban Environment
ISBN 978-1-58948-082-7

Smart Land-Use Analysis: The LUCIS Model
ISBN 978-1-58948-174-9

ESRI Press publishes books about the science, application, and technology of GIS. Ask for these titles at your local bookstore or order by calling 1-800-447-9778. You can also read book descriptions, read reviews, and shop online at www.esri.com/esripress. Outside the United States, contact your local ESRI distributor.